Black
Buddhist
B-Boy
& Beyond

*"The old shall be renewed,
and the new shall be made holy."*

— Rabbi Avraham Yitzhak Kook

Albion-Andalus Inc.

P. O. Box 19852

Boulder, CO 80308

albionandalus.com

Design, composition, and cover design
by Albion-Andalus Books

ISBN: 978-1-953220-41-7 (PB)

Manufactured in the United States of America

Black Buddhist B-Boy & Beyond

KYVA HOLMAN

Albion Andalus
Boulder, Colorado
2024

Dedication

This book is dedicated to my number one long-term fan and supporter, my father: Alvis Jay Holman Jr.

Author's Note:
Wha Haa Happind Wuz . . .

This book was mostly written over a two-year period between 2017 and 2019, after being initially inspired by a prompt on the subject of 'hybridity' from one of my Naropa university professors, Bhanu Kapil. When my eyesight took a sudden and dramatic turn for the worse in 2019, and the COVID pandemic ensued, I was forced to abandon the project. In the spring of 2021, the professor leading my thesis-cohort, Netanel Miles-Yepéz, encouraged me to finish writing it, and, as the owner and operator of Albion-Andalus Books, agreed to publish it when completed. In spite of having lost my eyesight and consequently the ability to write, I was able to complete the manuscript with assistance from Daniel Jami, an editor at Albion-Andalus.

As cleanly and righteously as I have tried to live—spoiler alert, it worked—it's still very difficult indeed to be as honest and vulnerable as I have been in this narrative, and continue to be in my everyday life. Now that you're holding it, I might as well go ahead and tell you, cliche as it is, it's my baby. And as you shall soon discover, its baby mamma is none other than the Eschaton, the Apocalypse, the End of Days, etc. Accordingly it's a big hot mess. It starts with me as a 48-year old university student in 2017, traces back through my early life and experiments in Hip Hop, and follows my life forward, in a scattershot fashion, to the present. You're welcome, or my bad. As the good brother Common said *"One day it'll all make sense."*

Introduction: 2017

The bad news is you're falling through the air,
nothing to hang on to, no parachute.
The good news is there's no ground.

— Chögyam Trungpa

After eight years of Obama, Donald Trump's America feels very much like falling through the air with nothing to hang on to. An increasing inability to distinguish 'fake news' from factual data about the world as it's really unfolding both mirrors and feeds a sort of schizophrenic break in the collective consciousness of the body politic. The individual diagnosed with schizophrenia thinks, feels, and behaves 'abnormally,' due to a failure to make out what is real. False beliefs, confused thinking, anxiety, depression, substance abuse, 'hearing voices'—are these not readily displayed in any and every corner of society we care to consider? Technology, politics, economics, culture, ecology, and beyond churn together in a perfect storm, whose ultimate effect is *boundary dissolution,* as peoples and fields are being brought closer together by increasingly rapid globalization. Whether we like it or not, we're quite literally 'all in this together.' When the individual schizophrenic break is successfully managed, the result is shamanism: an ability to navigate material and nonmaterial domains. When the break is poorly managed, the result is institutionalization or worse. As society tries to manage its mental 'break,' this book is an attempt to come to grips with my own portion of our collective schizophrenia.

The original title of this effort was "A Black Bostonian B-Boy Buddhist in Boulder," intending, as I was, to drive home a point about the high strangeness convergent in my life at age forty-eight. I'm also having a very 'Gen X,' classic Sesame Street-ish, preoccupation with the letter 'B'— the way it erupts from the mouth, with such ferocity that conversation-stymying flying spittle becomes a very real danger. Bees feel like power when spoken mindfully, which is one of the reasons I find calling myself 'Black' agreeable; these days, necessity dictates subtler expressions of power. At the same time, that string of bees feels unwieldy for a book cover, and potentially problematic to talk about, for said danger.

And yet, it seems important at the outset to say something about what bizarre bedfellows these bees make as they present in my current circumstance. For example: to be a 'Bostonian B-Boy' is to occupy an odd place within the broader narrative of Hip Hop, which, of course, was birthed by African-American and Latino youth in the five boroughs of New York City. Like Philadelphia, Boston was a large East Coast city very much in the cultural orbit of NYC, which nevertheless, had its own thriving Hip Hop scene by the early 1980s, when I first became active in it. Nearly everything New York hip hoppers did, we did, even if six or so months later. Unlike Philly however, Beantown never quite emerged from the long shadow cast by New York Hip Hop; or at least, it hadn't by the time my rap crew and I left Boston for the Bay Area in 1995. Ridiculous as it may sound, I *still* carry an insecurity complex around this, even as I'm currently putting together music and lyrics for a new album.

Then, there is the issue of being a 'Black Buddhist.' There are a few very well-known ones—Tina Turner, Herbie Hancock, and Alice Walker immediately come to mind. After that, it gets murky. Angel Kyodo Williams, Zenju Manuel, Charles Johnson, Anthony 'Amp' Elmore, Jan Willis, the Venerable Pannavati, Bhante Buddharakhita, Lama Rod Owens, and a few others are holding things down. But Buddhism isn't anywhere near as entrenched in the African-American community as certain other traditions. The Wu-Tang Clan, particularly RZA, has from time-to-time espoused Siddhartha's teachings. But growing up, in terms of exposure to Buddhism, that's all I got. And I wasn't taken with the other religions I encountered more readily; my childhood run-in with Christianity left me confused and unconvinced, and an adolescent flirtation with The Nation Of Islam felt much more political than spiritual. But after a paradigm-rattling peak experience during a ten-day *Vipassanā* (Sanskrit for 'things as they really are') meditation retreat, I discovered I'd *always* been Buddhist, at least in attitude and orientation; from a young age, I innately recognized the connection between life and suffering, and regarded my own direct experience as primary. Buddhism has A LOT to offer a people who know something about suffering. It also doesn't require conversion. But the Dharma has some inroads to make diversity-wise, so one of my objectives for this book is to show the Dharma at work in the life of a black person.

I'm also 'Black in Boulder.' And believe me, *that* is a study in itself. Boulder's reputation for offering a high quality of life is in some ways well-deserved. High and dry, abundantly sunny, with the Continental Divide's mountain peaks and briskly running creeks, it's extraordinarily picturesque. Weed is legal, and that pairs nicely with the surroundings. In terms of the cultural milieu, it ain't Oakland, and it ain't Boston, although the hipster Buddhist website Elephant Journal maintains that Boulder is run by Californians and New Englanders. The Journal also gushes about how the city is so removed from the space-time-continuum, and how everyone is so healthy, well-fed, happy, eco-conscious, and leftist. It mentions in passing that the 2010 Census recorded the city's population at 89 percent Caucasian. And to be sure, Boulder is *blindingly* white. In fact, someone *just now* shouted underneath my window, "This is white America!" I couldn't make this up. Instead of reporting the conversation taking place within earshot as I write these words—the kind of commentary I often overhear at my window—I'll simply say that while it may be true that aspects of the 1990s and late 1960s live on here, there's a good bit of the early 20th century to be found as well. A few days ago, two people were talking loudly as I was passing by, well on my way in the other direction, and one of them said, loudly, "*It was like slavery . . . oh-my-god awwwkkkward!*" And the other, looking embarrassed, said, "*Oh-my-god . . . he's standing right there.*" A few weeks ago, a group of high school students crossed my path and, while walking past me, one shouted "'*Sup nigga?!*" to the great amusement of his friends. Are you SERIOUS? One guy flat-out called me a 'sexual offender'. . . for walking by. And I can't count the number of times I've walked into a restaurant or cafe where the conversations around me suddenly changed to 'Tupac,' 'LeBron James,' 'Obama,' 'Bob Marley,' 'chocolate,' and the like—punctuated with words like 'monster,' 'beast,' and 'animal.' We won't even talk about the clutched pocketbooks.

I could go on about weird combinations of bees: 'B-boy Buddhist,' or even, at this point, 'Black B-boy,' given Hip Hop's universality. But, hopefully I've conveyed the basic flavor of the thing. Again: what I'm getting at is how spectacularly strange it is to be tasked with this particular assignment of intersectionality.

This book, if I'm on-point enough, will track my journey here, from pre- to post-awakening (*Vipassanā*), and how I managed to not go entirely insane in the process—if indeed, I have. We shall see. And since I began undertaking this project under the auspices of a class at Naropa University, appropriately called *The Hybrid*, that is precisely what the book will be. And if I'm doing my job, I've already set a context for my particular hybridity. And what exactly is a hybrid? As a noun: a thing made by combining two elements, a mixture; as an *adjective:* a mixture, composed of different parts. Hence: Black, Buddhist, B-boy, etc.

Before I discuss how I intend to lay the material out, I should say more about how much of a hybrid I truly am. The year I was born has a lot to do with it.

In 1969, the world seemed to be unraveling. Of course, we could say the same of today, but that time was distinguished by the multiple, epic, open revolts and seismic cultural shifts dramatically taking place on every front. 'Civil Rights' exploded into 'Black Power', and suffered a bloody onslaught on that account; feminism, indigenous rights, and LGBT rights came onto the scene, and revolutionary skirmishes broke out in cities across the planet. The counterculture made it cool, if not mandatory, to drop out of the system, and it's hard to exaggerate how terrifying this was to the 'establishment.' You had Todd Gitlin's *Days of Rage* going on, campus riots, moon landings (supposedly), hippie mass murders, epic bands dissolving, disastrous mega-concerts, and much more. I was born into a maelstrom—the very beginnings of Western civilization's schizophrenic existential crisis—which of course continues and accelerates in our time.

As a child of the 1970s, I absorbed a stridently funky, 'afro-futuristic,' black nationalist attitude from a supernaturally loving, highly eccentric, musical family. 'Naturals', braids, lava lamps, abstract African art, incense and palm-sized, yellow, manila baggies all day. You black Gen Xers *know* what I'm talking about! Once, during a rehearsal for one of the many bands both sides of the family came together to form, somebody shouted: "*Hey Kyva! Come over here and play these congas!*" Before I could protest, somebody else snatched me up and plunked me down in the seat vacated by the breaking conga player. I must've been around six or seven. Overcome initially by fear, the band fired up a groove, and I shocked myself by immediately and intuitively locking in. "*Yeah, that's it! That's baaad!*" Music was never the same.

Concurrently, the radically altered social order of the late 1960s had been translated into perhaps *the* definitive television show for Gen Xers, Sesame Street; many, like me, were glued to the television set every time it came on. It's almost as if counterculture intellects, realizing the system was not going to yield, launched the landmark show as a last-ditch effort to save the revolution's bacon: "At least we can get the kids, man!" As an adult, I came to realize and appreciate how profoundly, subtly, and subversively deep the program was, how it was all along cleverly seeding its young audience with a utopian vision of color, diversity, opportunity, joyous exploration, cooperation, creativity, and ecological stewardship. Humans, talking frogs, giant birds, prehistoric elephants and monsters, each personified some aspect of the psyche (gluttony, misanthropy, neurosis); and they were all living, learning, teaching and caring for each other in a love-filled, if run-down, New York neighborhood. Doesn't that sound a little. . . stoned? Seriously! Go back and watch some classic episodes on Youtube if you don't believe me. The message becomes clearer, I suspect, when one compares the original with the modern version of Sesame Street, which has been stripped entirely of its quasi-psychedelic, leftist utopian subtext.

Then, of course, Reagan got elected and things went batshit. The 1980s were about as cruel a hatchet job as could be devised for a generation raised on so much optimism; we were bombarded with unvarnished corporatism, greed, mass layoffs, race-baiting, swindling banks, satanic ritual abuse, insurance homicides, etc. After six years of school in a vigorously racist Boston suburb, and the devastation of Roxbury (my neighborhood), Dorchester, and Mattapan by crack, AIDS, Reaganomics, and apartheid—radicalization was inevitable.

And then—quite nearly literally bequeathed by sympathetic ancestors in some hidden realm—there was Hip Hop. Ah . . . drums to the rescue, just as in the days of old, "*to the beat, y'all.*" We had our marching orders. Well: not exactly, in the beginning. As much as I'd love to fly into a solipsistic drone on the culture's origins, it's for another time. For now, suffice it to say that what initially drew me to Hip Hop was not a chance to 'flip off' a corrupt and degenerate society. Like the joints I initially rocked to—like "Rappers Delight," and the lesser known, but no less def, 12-inch "Super Rhymes"—it was simply about expressing one's own personal defness, enjoyment, and notoriety; making a little money was just a remote possibility, albeit an enticing one. A youngster at Naropa University once asked me in class if I knew I wanted to be a rapper in the very early days. I told them, not being a rapper wasn't an option; like the mob quote, "I didn't choose this life: *It chose me.*" Throughout most of the 1980s, my participation in the culture wasn't terribly different from my immersion in afro-futurist family funk during the 1970s. Indeed, my rap group with two of my brothers and our cousin was a nice little spinoff of the family phenomenon into a newer genre, one explicitly driven by poverty. A lack of money for instruments, and budget-cutting city administrations removing music programs from schools, meant that, for my generation, being musical necessitated using whatever was still lying around, or cheap; for Hip Hoppers that meant microphones and turntables.

In the late 1980s, due to the realities listed earlier, which were of course ravaging inner cities across America, Generation X, across the racial spectrum, awakened to an urgent need to become political. For me, it was thrilling to recognize a vague commonality between pugnacious punks prowling around Kenmore Square and the B-boys and girls they rubbed shoulders with in crowded nightclubs. Tension was there for sure, but it didn't prevent certain provocative moments of solidarity from arising, especially in response to fun-trampling law enforcement. Anyways, any self-respecting 'conscious rapper' at that time, including myself, was *absolutely required* to be hip to the esteemed black-nationalist pantheon our heroic peers referenced: your KRS-Ones, Rakims, Big Daddy Kanes, Chuck Ds, et al. Pre-Internet that meant that you had to read, at least a little, which is tragicomic to have to say. Coming into contact with the 'canon' (*The Autobiography of Malcolm X, Soul On Ice, Black Voices, The Nigger Bible, The Blackman's Guide to Understanding the Blackwoman, Message to the Black Man, How to Eat to Live,* and decisively, Queen Mother Dr. Frances Cress-Welsing's seminal *The Isis Papers*) turned me, again, into a different person. And although time and age predictably softened some of my rougher edges, this was more or less who I was until my ten days at Joshua Tree National Park in 2003.

Vipassanā, essentially 'just the way a Buddha sits,' is, as the phrase suggests, the Blessed One Siddhartha's method for attaining enlightenment reduced to its barest elements: breath observation and sensory monitoring. In practice, it's deeper, MUCH deeper! I'll disclose more about this in a chapter dedicated solely to the incident, as it is the pivotal point in my esoteric under, over, and inner-standing, the master-key to my reality now. The Dharma, like the Dao, 'cannot be spoken.' But since I'm assuming my task is to try and point to the thing somehow, I will attempt to convey my experience with words, however insufficient that may be. My life, after my eighth day in the meditation hall, was henceforth permanently divided into 'pre-*Vipassanā*' and 'post-*Vipassanā*' phases; I was one person going in, and another coming out. To summarize this transformation: all my past hybridizations were revealed in and as a 'master plan'—a plan so excruciatingly brilliant in its execution that I could never have dreamed it up consciously. So, whose plan was it?

And it only gets stranger from there. Why? *Vipassanā* demonstrated, so clearly and cleanly, that I'd been Buddhist the whole time that I was compelled to crash-course myself through whatever insight I could get on the subject. I read the *Abhidharma*, Herman Hesse's *Siddhartha*, the writings of Nagarjuna, the Suzukis, Dogen, etc. From there, I was led to Alan Watts, Manly P. Hall, and Terence McKenna, and then to secret societies, alchemy, and ancient mystery schools. Do you see where this is going? In a plot twist worthy of a blockbuster movie (a good, older one), I was led back to the Nile Valley, the Mountains of the Moon, Ethiopia, Kemet, and Egypt—*black African civilizations*. Oh my! As it turned out, the so-called 'Afrocentricity' I'd heard so much about in my nascent nationalist youth was not deluded, feel-good, revisionist history with no scholastic merit, as it was portrayed in early 1990s mainstream media; afrocentricity was dealing with actual, if expertly hidden and/or distorted, FACT.

And this is the basis for the final assertion I will make about my hybridity at this introductory juncture: the previously obscured historical record suggests an unlikely, yet self-evident, collusion between a very specific group of blacks (the Moors) and a very specific group of whites (the Knights Templar, the Rosicrucians, etc.) to produce some variety of globalized epochal synthesis. I'm talking here about your basic 'New World Order.' And I'm putting it dryly as a matter of practice to avoid emotional hyperbole, over what appears to be a gigantic 'grand experiment' to which the entire human race has been unwittingly exposed. Or perhaps *wittingly*, if perceived from a karmic/ reincarnation point of view? Is civilization, maybe even humanity itself, some sort of cosmological lab project? A holographic computer simulation, genetically manipulated by extraterrestrial intelligences light years ahead of us? We do know that American Negro slaves, for example, were *bred*, literally. But for crying out loud—how far does it go? You may be feeling that we're about to fall down a rabbit hole of wild conjecture, but that's not my goal. And yet, we *know* there are well-established, highly secretive programs for atmospheric, agricultural, biological, and psychological engineering taking place. There are more than enough brain-busting mysteries surrounding how we came to be human, and what our ultimate engineered fate may be, but for now I'm only trying to speak to it generally, to show it as yet another element of my hybridity.

I've already established that a Black B-boy Buddhist in Boulder is, at the very least, a composite type of entity. If human genetics indeed derive from deliberate tampering, human or otherwise, and I am in some arguable sense the 'monster' people have referred to me as, then my successful self-realization depends on facing, accepting, and embracing 'monster-hood.' As irrational as that may sound, extreme times call for extreme measures. If, on the other hand, 'monsterism,' if I might coin such a goofy word, is a *projection* I'm accepting from some external source, then that's got to be discerned and embraced. The purpose of this book is not to make a final statement about such a projection, but to explicate and discuss it in the context of my hybridity. In doing so, I hope to demonstrate that it's possible to evaluate what is ultimately a spiritual developmental endeavor in a scientific manner.

For such evaluation, I've found the empirical approach of the *Tathāgata* most helpful; there are good reasons Buddhism is frequently referenced in conversations around, for example, quantum physics! When researching quotes attributed to Siddhartha Gautama, one of the first to pop up is one or another variation of: *"All that we are is a result of what we have thought; mind is everything."* Similarly, physicist Werner Heisenberg is frequently quoted as having said: *"What we observe is not nature itself, but nature exposed to our method of questioning."* And what is a "method of questioning," if not thought? This brings us to Mentalism— the concept that all phenomena (physical, psychic, and beyond) have their origins in the mind. This is difficult to argue against! THOUGHTS = THINGS. And if that's true, it makes a powerful case for defining and examining, to whatever extent objectivity is possible, periods, frameworks, or even 'operating systems' of one's thought over time. That is, if one is interested in being free from external control mechanisms. Where are the missteps? Where are the great leaps forward?

Here is how I intend to lay out this book. Best as I can tell, it's gonna be fairly unorthodox. Not that I've read everything published, but I can't think of any book I've ever read that could serve as a precedent for what I have in mind. Well, that's not entirely true: Frantz Fanon, bell hooks, and a few others have written powerful tomes that could be classified as hybridized, but not quite like this. I have *a lot* of words in my digital vaults: essays, unfinished books, lyrics, letters, and I plan to use that material to virtually reconstruct the mental terrain I crossed to reach here. Each chapter will give a date, beginning with my pre-*Vipassanā* life in 1996. There will be a rap verse, in italics, that I wrote during that time, and other prose from the previously stated categories will be identified and interspersed throughout. In as much as I can recall, I will offer some commentary on the broader socio-political forces acting upon my awareness at the time, and explore revelations about my thinking and psychic states in response to those forces. As I make my way to the present, I hope that a clear and interesting evolutionary dynamic will be in evidence, especially in regard to my pre- and post-*Vipassanā* mental orientation. The reader will see, with luck, just how this Black Bostonian B-Boy Buddhist in Boulder came to be as the result of encountering a deliberately enlarged sense of 'Self'—a 'Self' that is not the same as, and yet not separate from, the whole (as a wild monk comrade of mine aptly put it).

sigh Okay! I've set myself up here. Now, can I do it? Let's go on ahead and check it out. . .

1996

Homicidal rap ass niggas vomit the same shit as yesterday
Another lame hit will go to press today
Blow your chest away with the tec, get rec, snap a neck
Keep it real, it's all good, smoke a blunt, cash a check
Vice president of 'Asshole Records', whacking off his
Dick behind the desk, fantasizing 'bout the profit
Ready, to exploit another mad gory, sad story
Only to achieve his own personal glory
So I spark it, I'm not a slave to the market
Committed to the cause, designated as a target
By the forces that conspire to deceive and defraud
Original sons and daughters of the One True God
Nyambezi—the last of a dying breed
Too conscious to be a follower, too humble to lead
It's the power structure, I'm attacking
So I won't be seeking any institutional backing
Or corporate sponsorship, when I rip I represent
Self, squad, and black advancement
If there's hope for the wretched of the Earth to rise
Above their pitiful condition . . .
I'll battle to the death to realize
A miracle, spiritual evolution
The physical's not the solution . . .

In 1996, after a raucous second tour in Europe, my group and I were feeling mighty full of ourselves. European music fans are such a different breed than their American cousins that it's cliché to mention; and we were all, at least slightly, taken aback by how warmly we were received.

I'd been introduced to racial politics many years ago, when I was going into the first grade, through adult accounts of what *'them whiteys are doing to us in Southie,'* during the 1974 Boston school desegregation/forced bussing crisis. There's a chilling, infamous photo from that time, which encapsulates the conflict; in it, a black man (in a suit, mind you) is being physically restrained by one white man, while another clutches an American flag, aiming the tip of the flagpole at the restrained black man's chest.

The Exile boys and I had actually been in a scuffle with white townies at a traffic light in South Boston, then a predominantly working-class Irish enclave. On the other hand, in the early 90s we'd met, befriended, and collaborated with an all-white rap group, called The Sweathogs, from a similar Boston neighborhood (I can't remember if it was Chelsea or Charlestown).

Anyway: there we were in 1996, darting back and forth across borders, languages, and histories, performing to European audiences, in a subgenre we'd now call 'live band Hip Hop.' I should mention here that The Exile Society/ Triple XXX (me, Tranque, Hypno, LCJ, Jeff Langston, Stephan Mercier, 'Swiss Chris, Flueck, and Thomas Gromaire) were one of exactly three live band Hip Hop acts touring Europe at that time. The other two bands, at the time, were the Canadian duo Dream Warriors and The Roots, who of course went on to worldwide acclaim, becoming the house band for the Jimmy Kimmel Show. As far as I know, we three were the first.

During those two tours, in '95 and '96, the discussions I'd been having with surprisingly well-informed European Hip Hop enthusiasts began to erode my assumptions about race relations. Many of them were older and seemed to be upper-class. Some recounted attending shows put on by Funkadelic, Sly and the Family Stone, and Jimi Hendrix. Wherever I'd wind up—cafes, school basements, mega-concerts, cold water flats—I'd meet people with absolutely encyclopedic knowledge of American black music. Like those who came before us, we were regarded somewhat like visiting royalty.

We'd played nights with some very significant figures of 20th century African-American music, all of whom were critical acts in Hip Hop's early history: inventor of slap bass and former Sly Stone band member, Larry Graham, The Sugarhill Gang, Melle Mel of Grandmaster Flash and the Furious Five, and Bobby Byrd, James Brown's faithful sideman (who I sang on stage with for a few unfathomable moments). In fact, one night before a show, I sort of cornered Melle Mel, who was probably the first truly conscious rapper, with groundbreaking joints such as 'The Message;' paying homage to his influence, I subjected him to a barrage of new-generation lyrical science. Like, "Yo, Melle, check this out."

> *Fuck a NorthFace, I wear my war face*
> *I tell these young niggas that your place*
> *Be on the side of the dominant man before race*
> *Controlled world politics*
> *Battle-scarred, fuck a sellout kid, I never call it quits*

Although he was thoroughly unimpressed, with a smirk on his face the whole time, after patiently indulging me, his response to my winded coda was simply, "It's all good!" Huh? Like equal to a small bowl of turnip soup or a cracked frisbee? All good? Damn. Clowned! So my preconceived notions of inherent solidarity with awake, black emcees also began to come into question. After evidence compelled me to believe that meaningful cross-racial relationships were not possible, that 'all we got is us,' the uncritical unity I assumed existed amongst pro-black conscious rappers was coming under scrutiny.

The first collective experience I had in Oakland, after relocating there from Boston with the Exile Society in 1995, and returning there after our first European tour, was a great jubilation over the verdict in the O.J. Simpson case. During the trial, I'd gone back and forth with myself and others about whether or not he could have committed the murders. Now, after the verdict, black folk that never paid me any particular attention were randomly giving me daps and hugs as I walked down the street. People were honking their horns and shouting, "He's free! He's free!" As emotionally satisfying as this community joy was, I was dealing with some serious cognitive dissonance around it. Not only was there a nagging sense that O.J. may have actually done the crimes, and that black people were celebrating his exoneration despite a sneaking suspicion that he was actually guilty, but I was also bothered by the fact that we were celebrating someone who'd never championed black people. As Jay-Z's controversial song *The Story of O.J.* suggested, the brother had abandoned his racial identity a long time ago. But then, when he was in trouble, he was suddenly black again. And we rejoiced in his release because, more than anything else, a black male had for once prevailed in a patently racist, dysfunctional court system, which condemns black people as a matter of everyday business. As the Ruthless Rap Assassins said, 'There ain't no justice. It's *just us.*'

The following year, in 1996, Tupac was killed; probably more accurately, he was assassinated. Tupac Shakur, like the Beatles, is a subject over which so much ink has already been spilled that it's hard to imagine what there is left to add. Due to his larger-than-life legend, I'm assuming the reader will be, at least tangentially, familiar with some particulars of his life and thought: his impoverished upbringing and Black Panther mother, the fact that his youthful revolutionary ideology was intertwined with art and music, and that he once saw Hip Hop as a tool for black liberation. His trajectory and mine had some slight general similarities; for example, my dad was once a Boston field organizer for the Student Nonviolent Coordinating Committee. But as we go further into the particulars of hit records, groundbreaking films, superstardom, shootings, rape charges, and being a focal point in a cultural war between American coastal regions, the similarities end abruptly. And to be a Bostonian conscious rapper in Oakland, California in the mid-to-late 1990s certainly complicates any personal comparison.

The Exile Society, inspired by tales of 'hood entrepreneurs selling thousands of units out of car trunks, was an East Coast group trying to get put on in a West Coast milieu. Music purists, 'nerds,' if you will, (and I guess I may be one), know that regionalism and rivalry have been aspects of black American music for a long time—arguably, since the very beginnings of American popular culture, via spirituals, jubilee singers, blues, etc. But George Clinton taunting Kool and the Gang, Earth, Wind & Fire, and others to "Take it to the stage, sucka!" is far removed from musicians actually pulling guns on each other. But for that matter, I don't know of any incidents in which Tupac, or his slain East coast rival Notorious BIG, ever personally aimed a weapon at anyone. It was their respective entourages who enacted the threats Tupac and Biggie issued against each other, egged on by a scandal-loving corporate media, which gleefully poured gasoline on the flames.

My feelings about Tupac as a lyricist are probably about as consistent as he was. Unsurprisingly, I felt him when he was spitting lyrics on songs like "Trapped", from *2pacalypse Now*, and was appalled at the riotous divisiveness of a song like "Hit Em Up." Stylistically, in my opinion, he was no Nas, Canibus or Ras Kass. Still, as a Boston conscious rapper, in a town which put 'Pac onto this mysterious force called '*tha Game*'—not to be confused with the rapper 'The Game'—he was certainly provocative and important for me to consider.

In a Youtube video, Tupac speaks about living in Baltimore and New York City, before meeting up with *tha Game* in Oakland, where as he says, "All it take is for a muthafucka to be original." *Sigh* *If only*. It was, after all, *tha Game* that magnetized the Exile Society to the Bay Area in the first place. But although our quirky style put us in circles with other 'alt' Oakland acts (i.e. not exactly 'town business' rap), like The Hieroglyphics and Boots from The Coup, we never achieved the collaborations that might've given us more shine. There are several reasons for this, which mostly boil down to us not being local, and not having the proper attitude, resources, and equipment to play *tha Game*.

In 1996, I was very much contemplating the darker dimensions of *tha Game*, as it pertained to terms and conditions under which a black male might be permitted to see any kind of success in America. The prognosis wasn't promising. Then, as now, the folk wisdom was that there were more or less two avenues the average African American could take toward financial independence: music and sports—both of which led through the entertainment industry, and involved making unforeseen concessions, or rather, *sacrifices*. Tupac Shakur and O.J. Simpson were the subjects of many conversations in 1996, but while their money and fame was readily displayed, there were untold hordes of rappers and ballers who'd been enticed into *tha Game* and suffered heartily for it. I considered my life, at that point, to be inseparable from Hip Hop. And as a self-professed revolutionary, 'selling-out' was just about the worst thing an emcee could do. But that's what rappers were doing all around me, en-masse. Even today, thinking about these things causes a twinge, and I had to give myself a walk/meditation break to continue writing. *deep inhale*

The verse at the beginning of this chapter was a terse summation of my position on rappers who signed up to poison the black community for personal gain by peddling toxic substances and ideas, all while only collecting a pittance of their actual earnings for doing so. For those who may not be exactly following me: Hip Hop culture + the recording industry = rap music. Corporate products, which are what major label rap records are, exist to serve the needs, desires and whims of the '1 percent' at the top of the wealth pyramid. To say that their needs and desires differ from those of the communities most rappers come from is an understatement. Now, this is one of those moments to possibly fly into a conspiratorial rant. But again, the point of this book is not to argue conspiracy theories, but to discuss and contextualize hybridity. Although, that's not to say conspiracies don't exist; they very much do.

As I previously suggested, certain conspiratorial activities may even be, to some extent, clandestinely *promoting* human hybridity. We know, for example, about artificial intelligence, cybernetics, transhumanism, cloning, and gene-splicing. As to the "forces that conspire to deceive and defraud original sons and daughters of the one true God," I'll simply say that there's a whole genre of Youtube videos exploring and exposing the deliberate corporate manipulation of Hip Hop, and most other forms of popular music, which can be found with search terms like 'Illuminati music industry,' 'artists who sold their souls,' and 'rap occult sacrifice.'

1998

Now I love that dirty water, Boston, you're my home
I'm in a Bean state of mind, while I'm spittin' this poem
Better known for slangin;
Clam chowder, baked beans and pork
But out of town thugs prefer to call it 'little New York'
For your own comparison, follow Washington or Harrison
South of Mass Ave, where neighborhoods become a garrison
The way they fortified the block, you're mortified to walk
For fear of being killed in turf wars ordered by the cops
Executing mandates provided by
The Information Center, in South Boston
Delighted plus excited by the prospect for bloodshed
As long as it stays in Elm Hill,
Academy Homes, and Homestead
The old heads, remember Dudley Square
When it was lovely there
Soul food, bubbly gear, salons, get your ugly hair
Hooked up, but now cooked up rocks
Dominate the economic landscape
Even Grove Hall, the black Mecca couldn't escape
Mission Hill to Ashmont
Pint sized pharmacists get you whatever you want
The skyline is right there in plain view, all day
But from the hood it might as well be a million miles away

But kids are beginning to wake up, to take up the cause
Break up the claws of the beast, shake up the laws
Written to prolong the war to never cease
Big up to Wise Guys, NOI, and Gang Peace!

Reading these words back in 2017, I find them almost laughable. On the one hand, they sound inflammatory, like: "Man! No wonder I never caught a break!" But then I remember: I wrote this three years *after* I'd already left Boston. In 1998, quite simply, I was pining away for home.

Somewhere outside of Dudley Square, in an area considered downtown Roxbury, there is a small neighborhood, which is also a significant historical site, called Fort Hill. It's one of the neighborhoods my mind goes to when I think about the past. My aunty Kai, who passed some years ago, used to live there. As a teen, I couldn't wait for the rare opportunity to get to her flat. I remember how impressed I'd been by her lifestyle, when she invited me to party with her and her well-heeled clique. I think it must've been the first time I'd seen so many stylish, wealthy, and sophisticated African peoples assembled in one place. MAN! Champagne poppin', sparkly smiles, jewels, watches, suggestive hair flips, gentlemanly but spirited debates about city politics, sports teams, power suits, high fashion dresses—*haute couture* in full effect! And *everyone was black just like me.* The moral, though never verbalized directly, was abundantly clear: think abundance. There *are* black people living large, powerfully and assuredly moving through a hostile world. It took me a while, but I eventually figured out how crucial this was in my psychic development. Unlike too many of us, I was lucky enough to engage with dimensions of the black experience that inspired me to think beyond the hood.

As the name implies, Fort Hill is interesting for other reasons as well. It's the site of a military installment, cannon turrets and everything, built to protect Boston Harbor from the Royal British Navy's fury during the Revolutionary War. In my mind's eye, I can see the semicircular tracks in the platform where the cannon anchors, or what remained of them, were mounted. And I remember looking over Roxbury's urban density, and puzzling over how a cannon could have that kind of range, as I gazed toward the skyline—"Isn't the Harbor, like, a gazillion miles that way?"

It's hard to not feel at least a slight stirring when considering the epic story of America's foundation (especially if you manage to not remember the bit about slavery and genocide). I've always been something of an armchair historian, even before I over, under, and inner-stood history as mystery and 'my-story.' History was the one school subject, besides English, I knew I could excel in. And let me tell you: Boston's got history—colonial-era markets and graveyards, prestigious institutions, haunted stops on the Underground Railroad, and more! As a preteen, I remember looking at a miniature model mock-up of the Revolutionary War at the Prudential Center; you know the kind of thing I'm talking about, a nationalistic agitprop designed to make good patriots. Well, it worked—sort of. Crossing the Potomac, the rocket's red glare, I was almost down with it for moments. Then I discovered the 'Indians' of the infamous Boston Tea Party were white people in redface, and I remembered slavery. "Oh yeah—how could I support this? *I'm not a part of it . . .*"

Except, I am a part of it! Boston's complicated. And that's why I'm down with it. Or more accurately, that's why I came to be down with it as an adult, many years removed from being a resident. As racist, and well-known for it, as the city was when I was living there, its history has no shortage of prominent and important African Americans who have called it home. For example, many will have heard about the great patriot Crispus Attucks, who history remembers as the first person to die in the American Revolution. Patriot and abolitionist Prince Hall (evidently it was possible to be both) encouraged slaves and free blacks to join American's revolutionary cause, and went on to found black Freemasonry (another whole study in itself and potential rant point). Phyllis Wheatley, the first published and acclaimed American black female poet was a Boston resident, as was Fredrick Douglass, who hopefully needs no introduction. A less familiar figure, David Walker, a militant antislavery activist and orator also lived in Boston, as did the abolitionist and educator Susan Paul. In fact, the African Meeting House on Beacon Hill, where abolitionists congregated, can still be visited. Another Bostonian, William Monroe Trotter was a champion of Civil Rights, a newspaper editor of the Boston Guardian, a critic of Booker T. Washington's accomodationism, a real estate businessman, and the namesake of the elementary school I attended. The Right Reverend, Dr. Martin Luther King Jr., and Coretta Scott also lived in Boston; and the Doctor led a march from Roxbury to the Boston Commons in protest of segregated schools. The schools of course did desegregate, leading to the 1974 bussing melee I mentioned earlier, in which I was bussed to Reading for junior high and high school, through the METCO program. Thanks,

Doc, Malcolm, and Louis Farrakhan! As depicted in Spike Lee's "X", 'Detroit Red,' as Malcolm X was known at the time, once considered Beantown the hip place to live—that is, until discovering Harlem. I vaguely recall a story my dad once told me about ministers in the Nation of Islam discussing Malcolm X's assassination at my grandfather's house; and there are other stories in a similar vein. But all of this points to the fact that, as historian Daniel M. Scott III says, "Boston played a major role in black cultural expression before, during, and after the Harlem Renaissance."

But of course, the most direct and crucial impact of coming of age in Roxbury was being able to look up and down Humboldt, Elm Hill and Talbot Ave, at Dudley Square, Grove Hall, and other areas, and be reminded of the urban desolation found in the Bronx, Harlem and Brooklyn. The sprawling tenements, abandoned buildings and vacant lots of inner-city Boston in the 1980s gradually became a potent and inspiring reminder that we were indeed from the same socioeconomic conditions our heroic Hip Hop idols came from (just in miniature). I was proud to be from the war zone! Hell: I SURVIVED. But is that maybe P.T.S.D (Post Traumatic Slave Syndrome)? Whenever I get around to recording this album that I'm sitting on, "Boston: As Raw As Any City, Kid!" (or, interestingly enough, B.A.R.A.A.C.K.), I'll have some 'tales of the Lower East' to share; just to make the point that Bean was mos def in *tha Game* from the get-go, even if out of town thugs did literally call it 'Little New York.' I used to kick it with them, freestyling, politicking, drinking, and puffing on South End brownstone stairsteps 'till the wee morning hours. Ah! *"Memories . . . in the corners of my mind . . ."*

By 1989, my mother and father had moved the family to Boston's South End, and out of a rapidly failing community. I deeply regret having to put it that way, but that was the thing 'as it was.' American ghettos had intentionally degraded conditions and were pummeled by crises; but those same ghettos also spawned an earth-rattling response of athletic dance, record crossfading, top-to-bottoms, and stadium anthems—the art forms that would together become globally known as Hip Hop: breakdancing (b-boying), DJing, graffiti, and emceeing.

Ceding the floor to the experts, on their website, the Universal Zulu Nation defines the five elements of Hip Hop as such:

1. Graffiti is the writing of language, or the scribe that documents the history.
2. Emcee is the oral griot, the conveyer of the Message.
3. DJing is the heart beat, the drum of the art or movement; DJ comes from the Djembe drum.
4. B-Boy/Girl is the exercise and the human expression through dance or body movement to keep the body in proper health.
5. Knowledge is the reason why we are who we are where did our roots comes from, what is the beginning of Man and where are we today. How do we take the artistic expression of Hip Hop and find our purpose in LIFE!

We've arrived now at another probable rant point. Here's the thing. These days, it's easy to miss how deeply and radically transformative Hip Hop has been within the context of world history; that's right—WORLD history. In fact, within the culture, it's folk wisdom that Hip Hop is more alive and intact in other locales across the globe, than it is in the US. But this is largely underappreciated because the talent is not, and never has been, in control of the message—corporations are. And their interests, as I said earlier, are very different from those of the communities rappers often come from. But thanks to the internet, one can research as much as they can tolerate, to discover for themselves how vastly influential Hip Hop has been, and continues to be today. I know this because the culture continues to impact me. As I'm writing this in public, I've got the Slum Village Pandora internet radio station sending out morphogenic waves of vibration, with some appreciable effect on what's happening around me. Such is the compelling energy of the music—intricate, thoughtful lyrics and atmospheric, evocative tracks—conveyed from the past into the current ambient environment. And I'm hardly alone. Many of my generation have fallen, but many of us remain. Conversations and posts across the internet feature legions of 'old heads', Gen Xers and older, doing the same thing as me—allowing the music to continue inspiring and propelling them, as it did decades ago. Old school stand up! Hah! Dopeness.

How does this all tie together? At some point in the mid-1980s (right around the time of Run DMC and Aerosmith's smash, *Walk This Way*), more and more lyrical gladiators from urban war zones were beginning to be recruited by record labels with promises of profiting from *tha Game*. I don't know how many aunts were necessarily involved; but, apparently, plenty of A&R (Artist and Repertoire) people started exposing financially untutored people, without endowments and inheritances, to lavish environments, like the one I'd experienced in Fort Hill, Roxbury. If we recall that our subject is hybridity as it relates to evolution, it may become evident that I'm alluding to a process of poor people being fused, and infused, with 'rich notions and desires.' But—and this is important—what separated The Exile Society and I from a lot of other rap soloists and groups is that we were an extension of an intact, tightly-knit, loving family, that instilled us with a self-esteem that was not particularly reliant upon the opinions of others. Whether our peers lauded or loathed us, it didn't matter; we knew we were good. And I don't just mean we were dope emcees; I mean, we were moral and generally positive dudes. But not everyone was like us. Poverty, without a stable, nurturing family environment, and self-esteem, mixed with talent and enticement into *tha Game,* created the kind of rap content that eclipsed the positive stuff, which was carefully phased out through the 1990s. Yes, there were black people living large, powerfully and assuredly moving through a hostile world, but many had to make serious compromises in order to gain acceptance and access.

2000

The so-called 'classic European thinkers'
Decided every time a man tinkers
With the natural environment,
He adds value, creates order, and enhances
The cause of humanity, which elevates the chances
Of unlimited material gain,
To be supplied by imperial reign
Domination, competition, and mass production
All of which would go on to leave untold destruction
On the planet and people, no equal
To any period in history, no sequel!
Industrial Revolution considered the final solution
Never mind labor problems and to hell with the pollution
More machines, more products, more jobs
Would make kings and queens out of everyday slobs
But its first major achievement was world war
Impersonal manslaughter which set the stage for
The bloodiest century seen by mankind
With tragedy to stagger the human mind
All in the name of controlling the flow of energy, men'll be
Killing their mothers and whoever, enemy
Or lifelong companion . . . so here we are
With a bill for the party that we've had thus far
Every landfill is overflowing

A growing hole in the ozone that isn't showing
Unknowingly exposed to—radioactive
Rays that affect the human body
In mad ways that's unattractive
Polar ice caps melt raising the sea level
Even five feet and several
Cities and towns by the coastline
Are permanently underwater
You oughta see
Chicago and Las Vegas when they're beachfront property!
Deforestation corrupts a poor nation
But we lose too, when we refuse to
Replant the trees that generate the air
You can believe that your health is at risk
Just to breathe in the atmosphere!
And as the cost of maintainin'
The machines of business keep increasing and drainin'
The profits, companies downsize
Is it any surprise to see violent crime on the rise?
The Age of Progress left the world in a mess
And our days are really numbered, unless we address
The matter, unified and on a mission
A species that's determined to rectify a wretched condition
And realizing that everything that we do
Affects the next man, plant, and animal, but we're too
Caught up in the scrape for paper, to shape a
Adequate response to the rape of
The one and only planet we know that can sustain life
Guaranteeing that the time we have left will be short,
Trife and tragic, devoid of all worth

'Till eventually we're gone from the face of the Earth
And that means extinct—what makes a man think
It can't happen to him, when in the blink
Of the cosmic eye, it went down before?
I for one won't trip
When mankind goes the way of the dinosaur!

I think these lyrics are dense and detailed enough to cover most of what was on my mind at the turn of the millennium, so I won't prattle on too much about this one. But I will admit to being somewhat caught up in the frenzied hype over 'Y2K,' which some of you out there surely lived through; you know how it was! In short: the theory was that faulty coding, 'the Millennium Bug,' would cause the digital clocks in all the computers across the planet to turn over to 1900, instead of 2000. It was like the hilarious Simpsons episode, where the ball dropped on New Year's Eve and all holy hell broke loose—with Vladimir Lenin even rising up from his glass display casket like: "Must—Smash—Capitalism!" LOL! But seriously though, people went apeshit (seems a little familiar somehow). To make things worse, I'd just finished reading Jeremy Rifkin's bestselling, stupendous downer *Entropy*, which looks at societal structures through the lens of the second-law of thermodynamics, and argues that our fall into disorder, entropy, is inevitable, but made increasingly worse by our consumption habits.

In case you hadn't noticed: my thinking had, by this time, transitioned from a *sociopolitical* frame of reference, to a framework of *deep ecology*. This can be seen in the verse that started this chapter. It was from my first solo album

I Survived The 20th Century, and there were plenty of occasions for me to suspect it'd be my last. As appalled and terrified as I was to rap those symptoms of planetary disequilibrium, on the eve of a catastrophic computer meltdown, I was kinda amped too; I was excited to have lived long enough to see how it would all come flying apart. Fortunately, and somewhat hilariously, however, January 1st, 2000 came and went without the technology-addicted civilization collapsing in a great heap of sputtering electronic calendars. Although, significantly bleaker is the fact that many of Jeremy Rifkin's predictions, if I remember correctly, are coming to pass.

2001

I say 'Amazing Grace,' how sweet the sound
Maybe you don't think that's so profound
As for myself, I'm inward bound
To the shadows of my mind, see what's around
It could be black, could be white
Could be wack, could be tight, could be aight
On the other hand, I could be lost,
Never to emerge from that dark night
I'm a have to let y'all know, how it go later on
If I don't destroy my life, I'll be fly, word is bond
Better than I was before
Stronger, faster, more
Determined, hardcore
To win this hard war!

Oy. 2001. Talk about a rant point . . . I'm for the most part 'not going there.' Out of respect for everyone involved, and to keep my blood pressure down, I'm just not going to start with a polemic on 9/11. There are plenty of people on top of (lost in the middle of, and/or underneath) this very important topic for all of us.

I'd been doing collections for a black physician, a chiropractor for the city of Oakland, Medical Group at City Center. Pretty clean gig! I made decent money, and it was permanent; for a rapper supplementing his musical earnings with corporate employment, when not outright supporting himself on it, that was definitely a come-up. But what a strange, interesting office! It was like . . . I don't know . . . 45% corporate, 55% voodoo, with a lot of very 'top notch,' emotionally volatile black women, one prominent gay male provocateur, and a whole lot of sexual attention, and *tension*. I totally loved my reputation there—intellectual Boston nigga, accent and all, making phone calls and looking through files in the daytime, rocking mics at night, and practicing new routines on the weekend. (I'm currently listening to the Foreign Exchange's banger *Brave New World*, and these rhymes exactly describe my life at that moment!) Working class emcees, stand up! I also got a kick out of working for a wealthy black doctor and subversively undercharging and advising his economically distressed patients 'off the record.'

In the morning of 'the day under consideration,' I was drinking coffee and getting dressed, like a lot of people. In the middle of it, I got a hyped call from one of my coworker sisters: "Nigga it's *on* . . . turn on your TV . . ." And there were the smoking towers. I was swallowed whole by an abyss, while standing mouth agape, tumbling with no place to land, in the sunken place of all sunken places. After a few breathless exchanges, she hung up to call others. Then, seconds after, the phone rang again. This time it was my very attractive supervisor: "The doctor is shutting his practice down, and won't be needing your services anymore." Her voice was so matter-of-fact and measured; DOES SHE EVEN KNOW WHAT'S HAPPENING?! I hung up and said to myself: "Okay, this is *the end*. Well—let's see how it goes."

After absorbing the full density of the event over the next few days, I wrote the lyrics that start this chapter. By that time, I was just wrapping my mind around the new reality. The world as we knew it was effectively demolished. Bad as I knew things were, I had the situation wildly misconstrued, as we all did. If this was the level humanity had plummeted to, no matter who was responsible, a completely radicalized approach to the 'thing as it is' would be necessary.

Even though I'd called for a 'spiritual revolution,' I had no idea how truly dire one was needed until this moment. The urgency of everything was escalated. Did I, thousands of miles away in every sense, somehow bear responsibility? What did it mean 'to be of service' in a world like this? Who knew? But whatever it was gonna be, it required me to daringly gaze into and scrutinize my own darkness— the shadows of my mind. Some Jungian shit; psychological excavation—'CAUTION: Man at Work.'

And as I started this dive into my depths, I plunged headlong into the Bay Area scene of New Age 'encounter groups,' designed to bring the seeker face to face with 'the Other.' And that path led directly to and through *Vipassanā*.

2003

Breathe in
Breathe out
Take a second . . . to think about
What you would request, from the Universe if you could
For your higher good
Cause you can, and you should
Now more than ever
When mankind has worked so damn hard to sever
His connection to the real world, so clever
That now humanity faces total extinction
Courtesy of the weather
Building robots with human souls,
Tryin' to get them to set goals
To maybe one day take control
But they keep failing—cause they can't decide
On how to program things like vision, spirit, or pride
The stuff that makes us what we are
The ancient carbon from the inside of a star
In the midnight sky they seem many long miles away
But in fact, personified in you so why stray
From your true essence
Ever notice how moments of true presence
Let you know that you're working with like, a few blessings?
The lessons . . . are right there to be learnt

So many that at times you get burnt
There's so much in the world you can't make right
With any one individual fight, just look at the plight
Of people living on the streets or rotting in jails
Or hoods torn by war when wack foreign policy fails
Powerless, in the face of the AIDS crisis
Kids that die malnutritioned, blood rises
Vocalize this . . . if you can't contain
The pain, from the weight of the world and the strain
Now STOP.

Breathe

Visualize the full moon rising up over a mountaintop
The pale light, over the snow
Causes the peak to glow, and don't it look so . . .
Majestic, unexpected
Unscripted, in other words, undirected
Now let it fade to a beach scene
At sunset, admire how each green
Palm tree extends to the sky
While you're sitting on soft sand, cool wind, bird cry
Sitting down to your favorite meal
Appetizer, dessert, you got the whole deal
From the smell, you anticipate the taste
Knowing you won't let a single bite go to waste
In the arms of a dear one
So many problems in the world but you fear none
No jealousy, resentment
Just trust, gratitude, and contentment

So what am I trying to say?
Just this—every moment of every day
Holds the promise—if you're knowin' and seein'
Of the boundless, transcendent magnificence of Being
In this human form
Which is something that I've come to believe
That you knew when born
And believe me—I was the least convinced
The stars said it was coming; it's been on ever since
I doubted the magic: now my eyes are open
Plus I know it's where you focus, and you guys I'm hopin'
But nah, better yet, I'ma let it be still
Cause if you ain't feeling me now
I'll bet one day you will . . .

The preceding is a song I wrote to commemorate and contextualize what I experienced in 'the Main Event' of my adult life: *Vipassanā*. And since the best writing, by far, that I've been able to produce on the subject was an essay published in one of Itzak Beery's books, *Shamanic Transformations: True Stories of the Moment of Awakening*, I have reproduced it in full below.

Born and raised in Roxbury, Boston's equivalent of the South Bronx, or South Central Los Angeles, I thought of myself as carrying on the city's tradition of producing iconic black men along the lines of Crispus Attucks, David Walker, and Malcolm X. Having a dad who was a field organizer for the Student Nonviolent Coordinating Committee, during the time they were organizing into the Black Panthers, helped. He, as well as my mother, my aunts and uncles, and their peers, was also involved in various singing groups and bands. Coming of age and becoming politicized in the 1980s (Reaganomics, Apartheid, crack cocaine, etc.), it seemed destined for me to become a participant in the confrontational do-it-yourself subculture of Hip Hop. In the winter of 2002, on the eve of the most decisive moment of my life, I was nothing less than thoroughly identified with the persona defined herein: "*Sounds like fun, but 'some' of us are too invested in the hard slog of dismantling the institutional superstructure, fighting the power. I'm a gate stormer, a social reformer, or, in a time of momentous upheaval, a potential martyr.*"

As an inquisitor of apparent reality, I was not averse to deep contemplation and intense inner work, so long as it yielded instantly obvious, practical, real-world results. To my mind, action and conflict generated meaningful change. A meditation retreat felt a bit too much like New Age, psychological escapism: white, middle-class, indulgent, privileged, and indifferent to the cries of the suffering masses. What did sitting on a mat have to do with 'the struggle'? . . . "*I advance, not retreat.*"

But my ol' lady, a demonstrably psychic jewelry designer and daughter of classical Greek scholars, insisted I begin to meditate with her. And since I'd courted her (which was completely out of my character), on an intuitive hunch that she'd fling open peculiar and thrilling new doors of discovery and possibility for me, it didn't take a strenuous effort on her part to convince me to join her.

The meditation, situated in the high desert town of Joshua Tree, in Southern California, is known by its Sanskrit name of *Vipassanā* . Roughly translated, *Vipassanā* means 'things as they really are.' In other words, an immaculately clear perception of what is true at the deepest level. At the time of my arrival on the chilly compound, I hadn't a clue as to what the implications or consequences of 'things as they really are' might be, and whether or not the ol' lady had intuited anything she never said. As it turned out, ignorance, or more charitably 'beginner's mind' (in the words of the great teacher and Zen monk Shunryu Suzuki), was probably my strongest trait going into it. Being very goal-oriented then, knowing there was a specific kind of favored outcome would have caused me to seek it, instead of simply experiencing what came up naturally, which seems paramount to the exercise.

Learning the *silas*, the virtuous codes of conduct to be observed over the course of the meditation, was scarcely a concern. No killing, smoking, lying, or stealing? Hey, I don't do any of those things anyway! The instructions for *Vipassanā* were in fact deceptively simple: meditate, eat, sleep, repeat. No television, no reading, no electronic communication, no talking? No problem! These ten days will be a cakewalk, I thought to myself.

The first two days were a languid dream, in spite of a fairly rigorous schedule that consisted of hours spent sitting perfectly still and silent, watching the breath as it entered and exited my nose (or 'nostreels,' as the honorable instructor S. N. Goenkaji pronounced 'nostrils,' in his thick Burmese accent). With typical Capricorn conscientiousness, I attended every sitting, beginning at five in the morning, pushing through back and leg pain, boredom, sleepiness, ringing ears, other forms of discomfort from the cold, and periodic bouts of severe self-doubt. I was doggedly determined to give whatever was being offered a chance to manifest.

The first effect was a subtle shift in my sensitivity to time. Meditations, meals, and meandering aimlessly across the arid, stunning desert grounds felt less like planned, discrete activities, and more like a single flowing event. By the third and fourth days, bizarre things were happening with my body. Certain thoughts, mostly memories, would cause me to go into violent, and in the beginning, terrifying, convulsions. Invariably, these were visions of various women, only some of whom I had known, that I'd had unrequited sexual feelings toward. A puzzling pattern emerged: I'd recall a certain woman and immediately be wracked by involuntary spasms that I knew instinctively were related to past arousal, but which were not at all arousing in the moment.

Years later, I would come to understand that these were 'karmic knots'—energy blobs of sorts that get lodged in the body as a result of unfulfilled desires and cause unconscious suffering. As disquieting as these were, I resolved to redouble my efforts; something powerful was definitely happening. Concurrently, the dusty wind on my skin had a new tactile presence; narrow bands of golden midday heat felt . . . intentional, benevolent. Stars in the crystalline midnight sky seemed closer than I ever remembered them being. Every taste, sound, and touch was more densely packed with sensation, with exquisiteness.

I spent the fifth and sixth days confronting the absolute loss of my sanity. After crouching behind a bush to avoid a helper banging a small gong summoning us to the meditation hall—fearing an instinctual urge I had to lunge at his throat like a cornered animal—I thought to myself, "*Well now I've done it. I've gone and driven myself mad.*" When I finally did drag myself back into the hall, we were collectively instructed to mentally 'scan' our entire body, from the top of the head to the tips of the toes and back up again. Doing this, I discovered that the panging sensations had localized in the bottom half of my body, while enigmatic, tickling, swirling plasmas of sensation coursed through my torso and upper limbs. When Goenkaji predicted in his pre-recorded remarks that, "By now, you may be experiencing gross random sensations in one part of the body, together with subtle sensations in another . . ." my imaginative capacity was driven to its outer limits. "*What is this?*" I wondered. "*What's going on here? And how does he know?*"

On the eighth day, I took my place in the meditation hall exactly as before, fussed myself into an agreeable position for my back and legs, took some deep breaths, and began to scan my body. As if ignited by the turn of a key, the gross and subtle sensations began. And then, in the midst of these, which I'd fully come to expect, Goenkaji remarked: "At this point, you should pay attention to the spine . . . " Funny, I had not thought about my spine at all. When I did, all tactile experience as a distinct physical entity was sucked into my spine and ejected from the top of my head, as if pushed from below and pulled from above by unseen forces.

Okay. If I lived seventeen more lifetimes, I don't suppose I could summon the words to adequately articulate the state of awareness this particular set of circumstances left me in. But if I must make some poor two-dimensional overture to a sort of description, and my assumption is that one would be useful, I'd say that it was complete unmitigated liberation, a seamless merging with the 'Ineffable, Immeasurable Substratum of Being Itself.' All distinction between me as a perceiver and external objective reality disappeared. There wasn't a single passing millisecond that registered to my consciousness anything less than absolutely interconnected 'Oneness with All.' As above, so below.

Accordingly, I spent the rest of the day in a state of blubbering, incoherent bliss, like a newborn infant tossed before the overwhelming grandeur and sublimity of it all. Every character artifact of the distinct, separate 'I' that I had carefully constructed over the decades, all of my labels: 'black,' 'male,' 'Bostonian,' 'rapper,' 'intellectual,' 'radical,' 'Capricorn,' fell away like colorful, but lifeless, leaves. 'Kyva' had left the building, and couldn't be more pleased. In his absence, the distant mountains breathed for the first time. The scramble of life under the parched desert floor resonated. Each element—wind, sky, and earth—embraced as if greeting a long-estranged brother. Undulating tree branches pantomimed, "Hi."

Nineteenth-century scientist and writer Johann Wolfgang Von Goethe coined a phrase that seems apropos here: 'delicate empiricism.' Attunement to the ecology generates profound sensitivity. I thought: "How could the implicit order have been this premeditated, this sacredly and tenderly designed, this baldly obvious the whole time?" Perceiving myself as a hapless fool for missing truths explicit in every minute, I laughed aloud at myself. What a misunderstanding that was!

In the long run, this experience upended every conceivable dimension of my existence. When I've attempted to have others help me define what I experienced, and determine whether it was *nirvana, samadhi, satori, jnana, kundalini* rising, or some other phenomena, I've had no luck. Thus, I'll just call it an awakening, albeit one that has provided a fully substantiated master narrative for my life. Everything I've been through thus far hangs together in a coherent chronicle. My suspicion is that a 'good story' (and I realize now that that's all it really is) is pivotal in matters of self-actualization and finding one's true purpose. I've tried several times to build a manuscript recounting this narrative, but I always feel like I'm leaving critical details out of a still unfolding plot, and still do even as I present this retelling. Stages and events in my life now fall into two basic categories: pre-*Vipassanā* and post-*Vipassanā*.

Before *Vipassanā*, I was moving in the direction of edification, but hadn't yet found my 'X factor,' to use a hackneyed, but concise, meme. I had what seemed to be vague inklings on where to search, although looking back in hindsight, these were actually pretty exact. When an opportunity presented itself to me, to participate in something that felt important, but guaranteed no concrete outcomes, I took a risk; and trusting my inner promptings and the integrity of the company I was keeping, I pushed past my comfort zone. In the midst of riotous psychophysical reactions, I stayed calm and redoubled my efforts, trusting again that there was an intelligible, benevolent logic at work. The payoff absolutely surpassed anything my imagination could generate.

My post-Vipassanā lifestyle can be summarized as what philosopher Ken Wilber has called 'transcending and including'—simultaneously being whole and part of a greater cosmic whole, yet also integral to the natural world and grounded in basic animal physicality. All my ethnocultural affinity remained, but it was mediated by wisdom revealed through the prophetic visions of seers and saints. How fortunate it is that these have been passed down to shepherd our enlightenment in this moment when they're so desperately needed! And who knew? After years of fruitlessly trying to resonate with Christianity and Islam, it turned out I was Buddhist the whole time! No other religion/philosophy/way of life speaks to me so convincingly, so forcefully; no other strikes me as empirically reliable as Buddhism. Though this was my formula for transformation, I know it's hardly the only one. I'm fond of the axiom, 'many base camps, one summit.'

I had a new name that my ol' lady contrived for me: the black *bodhisattva*, which felt apt. *Bodhisattva*, in Mahayana Buddhism, is "a person who is able to reach nirvana but delays doing so out of compassion in order to save suffering beings." A *bodhisattva* employs whatever means they have at hand to assist the awakening of others, while remaining conscious of the fact that each of us is as unique and indivisible as we are interconnected and familial.

Coincidentally, the similarity between a *bodhisattva* and a shaman is that both have powerful medicine gained in victory over some dire existential challenge (often internal) that they bring back to their communities. As I ponder the possible future of the state of California without an adequate supply of water, it's manifestly clear that the wisdom gained from both the healing of the shaman's 'core wound' and the bodhisattva's tending to the 'cries of the world' will be vital in ameliorating the grim situation we're currently facing. In the final analysis, sitting on a mat had *everything* to do with 'the struggle,' for it raised my personal ecology of meaningful change above anything that could be called 'struggle' in the first place.*

Many modalities have taken me deep into the 'shadows of my mind': unconscious (Jungian) art therapy, water therapy, sound therapy, gem therapy, pranic energy healing, vortex healing, *reiki*, Subud, 'rose' reading, hypnotherapy, aromatherapy, Big Mind Process, Ipsalu Tantra, tarot, astrology, kirtan, astral projection, the Enneagram, martial arts, deprivation tanks, sweat lodges, Swedenborg, various churches, and a half dozen others I can't remember. I even gave Scientology a quick once-over; um . . . no. I'd always thought I was cognizant of how my psyche was influenced by the sociopolitical, economic, and cultural effects of white supremacy and 'Post-Traumatic Slave Syndrome' (although I didn't have that language until around 2007, after Joy De Gruy's groundbreaking book by that name). I knew I was *angry*; to paraphrase James Baldwin, to be black in America is to live in a constant state of rage. But as it turned out, the depths of that rage were unexpectedly extreme, seemingly inexhaustible in fact, and more than a little alarming. And who was I really infuriated with? For the first time, the 'enemy' was unclear.

I'd come face-to-face with a question that had hovered on the periphery of my awareness throughout my indoctrination into blackness: to what extent did I ask for this? Adults around me, family and friends, had regularly

*End of previously published essay in Itzak Beery's book *Shamanic Transformations: True Stories of the Moment of Awakening.*

referred to me as an 'old soul' as a child. For most of that time, I considered it to be merely a thoughtful compliment, although again, I didn't have that language: 'they're being 'nice' is all' was more like it. At the same time, why exactly would being called an 'old soul' be a nice compliment in the first place?

There was a telling story my mother and father would recount throughout my youth—one which told them unquestionably that I'd done this many times before, and one which, I figured out later, in many ways, frontloaded my self-perception, on some ol' self-fulfilling prophecy-type shit. The anecdote has me, at two years old, walking with my father and feeding ducks in the Boston Commons. For some reason, he informed me: "You know, Kyva, sometimes people *eat* ducks." Hearing this, I looked up at him in horror, rolled my eyes, shook my head, and said, "See! That's why I *hate* people." LOL! Oh, word? At two, huh?

Among my favorite apocryphal tales about the Blessed One, Siddhartha Gautama, is his fateful rendezvous with Mara underneath the bodhi tree; and it's worth offering up a little of the context of this encounter. Some will recall that the young prince Sid sets out from his father's palace and is shaken to the core by the sight of an elderly man, a sick man, a corpse, and saffron-robed holy men. After practicing severe austerities with wandering forest monks, and damn near starving himself to death, the Buddha finally resolves to sit utterly motionless under a tree, until he has the answer to the question dogging him: why is there suffering? (The milkmaid who fed him is considered by some to be the first female ancestor.) This remarkable specimen of a tree can still be visited in Bodh Gaya, India, in the state of Bihar, although numerous trees have been planted to replace the exact tree under which the Buddha sat. Sometime after Sid assumes his meditative posture under the tree, the archdemon Mara appears in front of him. Determined to prevent him from attaining enlightenment, Mara summons a ferocious and terrifying army of demons and ghouls. All together, they launch a barrage of flaming arrows at the seated monk, but he merely gazes at them, completely unfazed. This causes the arrows to metamorphose into flower petals falling harmlessly to the ground. Mara then changes tactics and summons his beautiful young daughters to seduce the monk. He remains unmoved. Finally, in a fearsome rage, Mara shouts in the monk's face: "Who will ever believe this so-called enlightenment you supposedly get?" To which he responded, touching his fingers lightly to the ground: *"The earth is my witness."* The ground shook. Soundly defeated, the demon Mara dissolves into the ether, and prince Siddhartha becomes the Buddha, the Awakened One.

Starting with the Y2K panic, I had been crawling, spiritually half-annihilated, through the twisted wreckage of 9/11. Beginning with *Vipassanā* in the winter of '02 (oddly, I was age 33), I'd undergone a path-altering, mind-bending, gut-wrenching alchemical transformation I couldn't have cooked up in my wildest dreams, or most haywire nightmares, that culminated in the completion of my second solo album, *Enter The Black Bodhisattva* in 2006. By this time, I'd also identified a few strange and interesting parallels between the Buddha's awakening and my own *Vipassanā* experience. Although my family certainly wasn't economically wealthy, it was very much spiritually and soulfully rich. My dad didn't have a kingdom or princely title to hand off, but my relations regarded me as something of a golden child, born as I was into the demoralizing mayhem of late 1960s black America. And the demons and dancing girls definitely descended during my ten day retreat.

Like Star Wars, The Matrix trilogy, X-Men, or any number of modern-day myths, the power of Gautama's enlightenment tale lies in how easily a motivated and perceptive person can find within it themes that are resonant in their own life. And of course, Joseph Campbell named this as precisely the point of the 'hero's journey' archetype. The 'hero's journey,' condensed, takes place in the following stages: a call to adventure, refusal of the call, meeting of the mentor, crossing the threshold, enemies, tests and allies, approach to the innermost cave, ordeal, reward (or 'seizing the sword'), the road back, resurrection, and return with the elixir. Some, or all, of these can be included in any journey with possibly differing orders of occurrence. Or, for an even more abbreviated form of the same journey, see the Zen aphorism: in the beginning, when seeking the Buddha Way, mountains are mountains; somewhere in the middle, mountains are no longer mountains; and then, at some stage of practice sufficiency, mountains are mountains again. As with the 'hero's journey,' this aphorism describes traversing ordinary and unordinary worlds.

As long as I'm on the subject of stages and traversing worlds, Ken Wilber also talks about these things. He's been gracious enough to add some significant general orienting principles to our collective knowledge with his theory of quadrants, states, and stages; these are exactly what this book has been talking about. I don't necessarily need to unpack the whole framework here, but I will say, in summary, that individuals and collectives (i.e. society) have various possible inner and outer states and stages which, if acknowledged and worked with, can spur conscious evolution. Transcending and including—becoming more whole by simultaneously going beyond and keeping various individual and collective personality artifacts—is nothing if not a process of hybridization. His events are way too pricey for me (and I did consider attending them as a potential benefit of living in Boulder); but from what I've gathered from his free offerings and his ambitious book *A Brief History of Everything*, I've been engaging with his 'all quadrants, all levels' integral framework the whole time. He's pretty big on Buddhism and, in that sense, I'm right with him. Seems to me that a human hybrid-type situation is what he's after, and that makes it somewhat regrettable for all of us that he never 'goes there' in terms of African spiritual contributions, which are of course the ultimate fount of spirituality on planet Earth. But, you know . . . *WHATEVER.*

2006

I find myself . . . back in the world of the hungry ghosts
Of the, broken promises and empty boasts
Of the, karmic beings with imperfect hosts
Which we call the vessel, or the body, known to most
As the primary thing to satisfy, gratify
A million and one desires to pacify
Man I need a cigarette, where the Henny at
Where the weed at?
Gotta get paid, money I need that
Gotta get laid, or at least some kind of feedback
From the opposite sex, it ain't hard to see that
Suffering, is the nature of this existence
Everything else is buffering, or resistance
We're either—craving something, or pushing it away
What we don't want, we get
What we want comes but won't stay
A true sign of growing, is when you're knowing
That all things are constantly coming and going . . .

Nyambez is on a quest to be immaculate?
Well I'm finna be the black bodhisattva's devil's advocate
Aight well check this, partna: is you up on your virtues
Like Number Seven, the Far Going,
You try to work through

Self-improvement? I see you;
What about Number Nine though
The Good Thoughts, Charity, leaving no one behind, yo?
And number Ten, the Clouded Doctrine, I figure I know
That you reached perfect wisdom
When I see your ass glow, though . . .

Brother Sir, you've learned well, so pray tell
Do you recall the hell
I got when I came back from Vipassanā ? (yup)
I stayed calm 'cause I had compassion
From being treated in the same fashion (huh)
To deal justly must be the course
Good karma that I gain with you, with the source
Being, the good will that was shown to me
I figure the best way to pay it back, is to try and be
a black bodhisattva . . .

In this verse, I employed a foil, a doubting Thomas, to help me illustrate the Way of the black bodhisattva; and the part was performed by none other than my brother and former bandmate, Hypno. Our group had been defunct for three years already, and by 2006, I was well into an obvious and unanticipated (though identified in self-realization circles) phase of falling away and dissolution.

A couple of years after moving to Oakland, we'd changed the name of the group to 'The Subterraneanz;' the label seemed fitting enough. As the Exile Society, we four were accepting and reclaiming our apparent outgroup status as pre-convicted 'thugs,' despite being good dudes calling for social change. Like, '*Yea we been kicked out, and what of it—*

there's a gang of us miscreants, so watch out!' (the proverbial middle-finger to the status quo). In tha Town, replicating our tendency to put on other emcees we respected caused the operation to balloon with new members and associated acts; and all of it was pretty damn subterranean—in the shadows, the underground. It was an exciting time—a new thousand year period; we had four tours of Europe to our credit, our first commercially available album, 'Subterranean Means,' in 2000, and a growing reputation in the Bay Area as an 'alt-rap' group to be reckoned with. But this reputation was beginning to cause stress fractures among the members. Because the Society never had any designated leader— our extended family had discouraged us from developing divisive 'egos' the way they had —our lyrical content was all over the map, instead of focused on any one subject. Some of us were political; some were street-oriented, some pimpish; others were 'old-school', and even Gothic. In hindsight, it became obvious to me that this made us notoriously hard to slot into stiff, preprogrammed, commercial radio formats and predictable ticket-sale-craving performance venues.

But when I'd 'returned with the elixir' to the band from *Vipassanā*, in early 2003, nobody was trying to hear it, and my appraisal of our dedication and potential turned much more critical. I'd already been shocked to discover, in the waning days of the meditation, how none of the participants could make sense of the experiences I was trying to share; all of their observations seemed so mundane—'my back was hurting;' 'I was thinking about my dog;' 'I was thinking about how the Rams were doing;' 'The instructions conflicted with my yoga training.' I assumed I'd at least have a sympathetic audience in my cypher. But hell, I might as well have been jabbing a finger in my dimple and twisting it with a toothy, shit-eating coon grin on my face and a daffodil in my afro. I wasn't ever clowned, but there was a deafening silence. In the tense hush, certain counterproductive themes arose to my awareness about the way we rehearsed. People would show up to practice stoned, drunk, and pissed off to give up their weekends. Before a mic stand went up, or an instrument was plugged into an amp, more weed and beer would come out, and the name-calling and card-pulling would ensue. It appeared to me, watching this as I was 'from the outside,' that there was almost as much arguing and dissing as there was playing. The ol' lady, who'd made *Vipassanā* possible, was already in my ear suggesting I go solo, which my bandmates knew and resented. As distasteful as I found her assessments, I couldn't disagree with them: "You're different now . . . you need to make your own statement . . ." Yeah, I know, John and Yoko shit; except I was no Lennon!

On December 7, 2003, a date which will live in infamy for me, until it doesn't, tensions finally erupted, and in one of the absolute worst times I've ever had, the band imploded. What a fiasco, and still another possible rant point! Things were said very uncharitably and unmindfully, and I include myself in this. The four founding members of the Exile Society had been together for twenty years at this point. We were supposed to succeed, where other bands the family put together failed because of EGO. And now here we were, "falling the fuck apart," as my irate brother put it, *because of ego.*

Everyone connected with and/or concerned about the career of the Subterraneanz was stupefied and saddened . . . except for the ol' lady. Well: turns out she was right— sort of. Three years later, I had finished my second solo album, 'Black Bodhisattva'—a compilation of songs I'd been recording since 2001. It's about as pro-Buddhism and anti-Bush as it gets. When Hypno and I met up to record his aforementioned part on the album, in 2006, kicking it with him was as bittersweet as the Cannonball Adderley version of 'Autumn Leaves' that I'm currently listening to, with autumn leaves literally swishing around underneath my window. Beginnings and endings.

Literally days after the band's implosion, I hopped on a plane and joined the ol' lady in Rajasthan, India. Like *Vipassanā*, she'd made it all logistically and financially possible. Generous lady! Also like *Vipassanā*, it took some convincing before I signed on for this trip—but not nearly as much as *Vipassanā*. It was India for Chrissakes! Mama India! To get the exact stones she needed to design jewelry, she went and sat with stone merchants across Asia; some of the Indians she worked with claimed to be descendants of stoneworkers who supplied the engineers of the Taj Mahal. Maybe, or maybe not. If you've been to India, you know exactly what I mean. Just disembarking from the plane, you step into an entirely alternate reality, where the world truly could be anything. The subcontinent, famously, leaves no visitor unchanged. With some effort, I could probably make the rest of this book about jaunting around there. Instead, I'll recount our visit to the Tibetan refugee resettlement camp in Bylakuppe, in the southern state of Karnataka.

Byalakuppe is allegedly the largest Tibetan refugee settlement camp in the world. Approaching from a long, winding, uphill road, the script of the signs lets the mindful traveler grasp that although the terrain may look classically South Indian, they are entering a region wrenched from its mountainous Northern space-time. I'd never been to the

Potala Palace or Dharamshala, but the colorful, organically baroque architecture reminded me of photos I'd seen of those places. I was particularly enthused to visit the Golden Temple, which, after *Vipassanā*, felt like a vital and predestined next step in the journey. I was in fact expecting to be greeted by the Tibetans as a long-lost brother from another mother, a sagely black anomaly from the West. The ol' lady and I meandered dreamily amidst saffron and yellow-robed monks piously spinning massive prayer-wheels, chanting, clutching malas, and walking briskly.

Sitting to rest next to some local ladies, at the foot of a stupa (one of several in a long, evocative row stretching dramatically to the horizon), one of them grabbed my hand and started stroking it with her thumb, while the others gathered around giggling and chatting in the local language. Seeing my befuddled look, the ol' lady remarked that they were, "seeing if it rubs off," meaning, my dark skin color. She said this after confessing she knew no Tibetan, and despite the fact that these women were damn near my complexion. It was part of a habit she had of periodically saying things to 'knock me down a few pegs,' and it took me years to imagine that there might've been other potential interpretations of the gesture.

Gradually, we began to tire of the food and gripe to each other about it; our diet consisted almost entirely of noodles with a few vegetables, some kind of meat, and yak butter. Novice haole that I was, I was also getting antsy about there being no hot running water. Then, our senses and sensibilities were assaulted by a late afternoon cafeteria scene of monks chasing, cornering, and beating down one of their brothers. The *peaceful, compassionate* Tibetans? Noticing what must have been our utterly horrified expressions, our servers assured us, laughing hysterically the whole time, that "he must've violated one of the precepts." But the crowning insult came when we finally made it to the Golden Temple. I sat in front of a giant statue of a deity, maybe Avalokiteshvara, for a meditation, to presumably, at last, put me face-to-face with the esteemed ancestors. What I got instead—the faint sound of clattering horse hooves, rising to a confused clamor of screams, swords cutting through air, and startling, grotesque images of bloody, airborne clods of earth, flying arrows, and disembowelment—could only reasonably be described as the Tibetan version of Hell. So thoroughly pummeled was I by the experience that I fell backward, passing out on the floor. When I came to, the statue's formerly benevolent eyes were glowering mercilessly down upon me, like: "You STILL think you're 'one of us'?" Well, not anymore. The whole trip had disabused me of the notion that one unclassifiable moment of direct-perception could automatically render me an ascended master with a cosmic world passport. The ol' lady had been kind enough to snap a flick of me standing in front of the statue looking disoriented and ashy, which in hindsight, I was glad she'd done, for the sake of documentation.

Getting back to the US in 2006, I put 'Enter the Black Bodhisattva' in front of the A&Rs I now had access to, thanks to 'the net' and the music industry website TAXI. They informed me that although they loved the arrangements, singing, and positive, thoughtful content, *I'd never sell it.* The material was simply 'too deep' for the Hip Hop audience. I might have better luck if I "took this hook out;" "I'm not saying 'dumb it down' but . . ." *E-yeah,* that was precisely what they were saying.

Fair enough. I didn't know how to 'dumb it down.' I knew, very generally, why the music industry censors were telling me those things (see the verse opening the chapter on 1996). Ten years after that verse, I was being forced to accept that the realities of *tha Game* were much colder, far worse, than I'd imagined. A decade after this, I realized it was all worse than I had the *capacity* to imagine.

And this brings us to the virtues that Hypno named in his part of the verse. After poring through the many numbered lists of Buddhism, which I didn't have the wherewithal to do in 2006, I now assume that he's referring to the Ten Bodhisattva *Bhumis*—the levels, or 'grounds' of Mahayanist (Great Vehicle) attainment. Number Seven is 'Gone Afar,' similar to, but not identical with, the chant "*Gate Gate Paragate Parasamgate Bodhi Svaha*," (gone, gone, gone beyond, gone totally beyond) of the *Prajna Paramita*, or Heart Sutra. You're not completely 'out there,' i.e. utterly liberated from the 'Wheel of Samsara,' the 'Wheel of Life Death, Rebirth, and Suffering,' but you're right on your way! I'll leave it to the reader to assess whether anything up to this juncture of the story sounds like going beyond. That's certainly what I thought I was on about. The ninth *Bhumi* is 'The Good Intelligence,' in essence, 'Right Thinking.' It is conceived of as a stage where the seeker is so masterfully aware of all possible worlds, scenarios, words, thoughts, and truths that perfect attainment is virtually assured, making one extremely peaceful and generous. I didn't directly answer Hypno's inquiry, "what about?" because whenever I was in his presence, I recalled how the Subterraneanz collapsed, and couldn't honestly call myself perfectly generous or charitable. The Tenth *Bhumi*, 'the Cloud of Doctrine,' is where the last vestiges of the false-self dissolve so completely that one becomes like a cloud passing in the sky, downpouring Dharma with 'Great Perfection' in all 'Ten Directions.' Hypno would be convinced of my attainment when he found me somewhere gleaming away in a soporific haze of perpetual bliss.

Oh yes . . . and by the end of 2006, my relationship with the ol' lady collapsed.

2008

Yes, I'm riding with Barack Obama
But if he's elected, is it expected, suddenly no drama?
I signed my name to the Fox petition
But if we truly hold this as a mission, it needs an addition
There's a saying: the government you get's
The one that you deserve
Cause at the end of the day, whose interest is getting served?
For all the complaining
There's gotta be a reason that the old paradigm is remaining
Picketing Fox is cool
But who's tuning into these shows that be a mad fool?
People want industrial farms to raise chickens, not poultry
But who dining at KFC?
We demand for human rights in China to play they part
While we strolling through the parking lot
Of Wal-Mart with a full cart
Bring the troops home at long last
And, oh by the way
We pay way too much at the pump for gas
Choices have consequences
Lifestyles create priorities—we need to come to our senses
I get around on the public transit
So I may arrive late, or not at all
But I'm willing to chance it

Recycle bottle, paper, cans, and plastic
Unplugged my refrigerator—damn, I'm drastic
So it's one vegetarian meal a day for me
Plus I pay 12 bucks a month to PG & E
Never got cable so a lot of shit I never see
With the exception of the Simpsons, mostly KQED
And the point here isn't 'nyahh nyahh nyahh'
But getting free
And it's far from perfect, but God willing someday it may be
You see, the bottom line is: too many people abide
In this freak-show carnival ride that ends in suicide
I'll leave you with this last question: what if one day
We all said "thanks but no thanks," got up,
And walked away . . . ?

When I first heard about brother Barry's candidacy, I have to admit, I wasn't exactly overwhelmed with enthusiasm. The only frame of reference I had for such a thing was Jesse Jackson's ill-fated runs in '84 and '88; and for me, politics in 2008, was more about conflict and protest than anything else. I also wasn't a fan of the Democratic Party, soured as I was by eight years of 'Slick Willie' Clinton's faux-liberalism and criminalization of poverty. But when it started to look like Obama had a legitimate shot at the office, I didn't exactly jump on the bandwagon, but I did begin to mildly advocate on his behalf.

At that time, I was back in the full-time employ of a black-owned-and-operated organization, doing client-centered collections in an Oakland milieu even more impoverished than that of Medical Group at City Center.

Again, there were the hot, emotionally volatile sisters, the sexual tension, and the East-coast musician mystique; but unlike Medical Group, this office was patently dysfunctional. Despite being consistently at odds with management, over what struck me as willful incompetence, I was good at what I did. I got the money and kept people happy, so I wasn't as disposable as they would have liked. Slowly, my cubicle became a lightweight Obama campaign center, where I sent emails and printed flyers from time to time. My position was not dissimilar to that of Princeton professor and bestselling author Dr. Cornel West, who'd said something to the effect of, 'Brother Barack, I *very tenuously* support your candidacy.' Though, I will cop to being into the whole Rev. Jeremiah Wright thing—it gave Obama some 'black bite.'

On election night, I fretfully toggled between news stations, monitoring the progress of the race. Finally, the announcement was made: "With partial results in, Barack Obama is projected to be the winner and 44th President of the United States of America." My initial response was like coming up on a powerful hallucinogen—for real; the time-space continuum rippled, and I was enveloped in a heady euphoria of relief, joy, optimism, and closure, along with a curious, thought-provoking surge of patriotism: "*Maybe this country really is 'all that.'*" BUT. Then I turned to public television, which was already blaring this thundering montage of fireworks, waving flags, depictions of slavery and Jim Crow America, and film footage of the Civil Rights movement, accompanied by a swelling, melodramatic score; and suddenly, the whole thing seemed very . . . contrived, engineered. It was like that moment in the second Matrix installment, where Neo mutters: *"It was all just another system of control . . ."*

However, engineered or not, the energy was inescapable. Images from Obama's first speech as president-elect are forever seared into my memory—masses huddling, swaying, sobbing, and clutching each other in the chilly night, and Jesse Jackson's tear-drenched face and quivering lip. It was a transformative moment in American and human history for a people greatly in need of a victory, a boost of confidence, and resolve. You could *almost believe* centuries, if not millennia, of karma could be wiped out in one blinding instant. And that may yet prove to be true! At that time, however, all that was appropriate was celebration. Accordingly, I jumped up and scrambled to 14ᵗʰ and Broadway to join the revelers.

Downtown Oakland was uproarious mayhem, and absolutely the place-to-be on the occasion: traffic snarls, people hanging out of car doors and sun-roofs toasting champagne, dancing on engine hoods, and leaping into each other's arms on the street. Everybody was laughing, singing, shrieking, howling, licking fake shots in the air; complete strangers were bear-hugging, terrorist-fist jabbing, and smooching each other—it was the most intimacy I'd experienced in years! Recall that Oakland is a city steeped in Afrocentric consciousness, most powerfully characterized, of course, by the Black Panther Party for Self-Defense.

Walking back home, I passed a dingy, obviously long-abandoned storefront on a downtown street and briefly stopped. Looking into the grimy, cracked front window, I saw what was only faintly visible in the orange glow of street lamps: dusty revolutionary memorabilia scattered willy-nilly—afro posters, statues, books, African prints, and Buddha knows what else. I also stopped for a brief contemplation of the Oakland County Courthouse, remembering scenes of leather-clad Panthers standing on those very stairs waving flags and shouting, "Free Huey!" (right around the corner from my flat—or 'Moby Dick' as it used to be called). *Um, e-yeah.* You couldn't live in *this* city and not know that an African American president—and one with such an eyebrow-raising name—was a BIG DEAL.

But was it really? A few days later, I saw a photo circulating on 'the Net' of the president-elect sitting with high-ranking military officials. His facial expression told a completely different story—no such change was forthcoming. His hair had already grayed. Now, you may be thinking that we've arrived at still another tremendous potential rant point, and you'd be perfectly correct. However, due to the fact that this ground has been covered by countless others, in far more agonizing detail than I care to summon, at this point, I will simply say: the issue of 'who's really in control' has been up publicly, *at least* since Dwight D. Eisenhower's chilling and ironic outgoing speech on the military-industrial complex in 1961. I'm no insider with privileged information to add to the discussion; even Youtube is utterly brimming with material on the topic. So, I won't 'go there' because, again, this book is about hybridity and reckoning with my own portion of our collective schizophrenia. What does seem useful to question is whether Barack Obama's eight years in office meant 'change has come to America,' but I'll take that question up later. For now, I want to briefly examine whether Americans were, or are, even ready for such a thing in the first place, as alluded to in the verse starting this chapter.

Off top: 'change' is, of course, inevitable, as the Tathagata made so abundantly and eloquently plain. The question then immediately becomes specifics: Change for whom? Initiated by whom? In what arenas? What exactly is being changed? What for? Who benefits? (And that last one is critical.) We have to identify from where the change is being *sourced*, from without or within. Who, or what, is causing the change? Us? Institutions? Forces beyond our control? CERN (The European Organization for Nuclear Research)? 'Principalities' of some sort?

From our spatial-temporal embodied circumstance, yes, change is inevitable, yet paradoxically, without a perspective like Siddhartha's, it is hard to engender, especially at a personal level. When people rally around cries for 'change,' I wonder if they're expressing a readiness *for* change, or a readiness *to* change. See what I did there? I strongly suspect many, if not most, people are ready *for* change, not *to* change; that is, they're down for change to be imposed from without, rather than consolidated within. To be 'ready for change' is passive, like: 'Okay, we have a new administration, so I guess we better get used to things being different.' To be 'ready to change' is active, and involves personal effort and internal resources of agency, will, and confidence; more like: 'The time has arrived for *me* to try something different.' Change is hard! No doubt about it; many possible mistakes and pitfalls will be there. So I can recognize and appreciate the reality of how tough it is to get with a process (change), which is inevitable, laborsome, filled with potential pitfalls, and guarantees no definitive positive result. The closer one looks at the situation, the more it becomes clear that energy is at the root of the thing; who, or what, has the energy to expend to make things shift? Much more highly trained minds than mine have carefully worked out these dynamics in advanced social sciences, like systems and game theory. And there's a reason money is poured into research and development in these areas. The problem (or advantage), well grokked in the social sciences, is that many will take the path of least resistance, and do as little work (i.e. expend as little energy), and assume as little responsibility, as possible. This includes not doing the work of, or taking responsibility for, discerning how the world really works. Television, movies, and social media are supplied, if you really think about it, to do the heavy lifting of opinion and outlook formulation. 'Woke,' or conscious, populations constantly refer to corporate-owned media as the primary culprit of creating artificially dumbed-down masses, the 'sheeple.' I empathize with that synopsis; I just don't wave my finger in anyone's face over it. I did in 2008 though.

From the rip, I found rhyming 'Obama' and 'no drama' typically witty. The verse starting the chapter is from a song called 'Mirror,' which had the chorus:

Take a short walk to the mirror
For a long gaze, til the image get clearer
You wondered where the problem was and where it sat?
Well look no further than that, that's where it's at
Come on
Take a short walk to the mirror
For a long gaze, til the image get clearer
You wondered where the answer was and where it sat?
Well look no further than that, that's where it's at

This song was indicative of a stage in my hybridization process, where I'd been forced to critically assess the idealized conglomeration I habitually called 'THE PEOPLE' (which seems, for all intents and purposes, to be a very 'leftie' framework). My early rap radicalism was, after all, informed by a late 1960s black-nationalist ethos, with roots in classical Marxism; although, 'I was not, am not, and have never been, a member of the Communist Party.' I'd spent most of the opening decade of the millennium agitating against the commander-in-thief, Dubya Bush, and his brazenly criminal and bloodthirsty Neocon regime. Over the eight long years of his tortured, illegitimate, farcical presidency, I became, more or less, a professional activist. I did it all: rallying, marching, chanting, drumming, boycotting, leafleting, study-grouping, speechifying, essaying, political sloganeering, songwriting, performing, debating, and arguing—so much arguing! I was directly involved in the multiracial, but mostly white, 'World Can't Wait' organization, and the, primarily Jewish, Network of Spiritual Progressives; plus, I politicked with members of the predominantly black Prisoners of Conscience Committee (P.O.C.C.) and the League of Filipino Students. In hindsight, this provided a useful, and perhaps unique, cross-section of exchanges to analyze the movement at large.

The theme which came to dominate my thinking at the time was: liberals are very ill-prepared to grok and take up integrating system-altering outer work with self-realizing inner work, which I see as an obvious need. Big up to the feminists who introduced the 'personal = political' narrative. I was well aware of the Left's materialist philosophical orientation. But for crying out loud—this was *the Bay Area*,

Northern California, presumably one of the most daringly progressive intellectual enclaves in the country. But as it turned out, there wasn't much in the Bay Area that dared to combine the inner and outer work. New Agers were New Age; leftist activists were political. Presumably, they wanted many of the same things: clean air, unmodified food and water, ecological stewardship, strong governmental oversight and accountability, strong voting rights, diverse and equitable workplaces, appropriate taxation of the one percent, historically marginalized voices in the national discourse, general compassion, etc. But moving in these circles, I never saw the political and spiritual overlap. Never the twain met. The activists were mostly grimly determined, the New Agers mostly blissfully insular. I'm not hating! I'm just saying. Rabbi Michael Lerner's Network of Spiritual Progressives was probably as close as I got to any sort of synthesis between progressive politics and spiritual striving; but being black, male, 'woke,' and from 'the streets,' it didn't feel vigorously confrontational enough for me.

As for the general population at that time, I remember a specific incident where the dimensions of the situation truly hit home. Sometime in '06 or '07, I took a desperate, two-day crowd control gig at WalMart for a 'Black Friday' shopping weekend. Oy! First of all, I never imagined Oakland even accepting a WalMart in its municipal boundaries; but it did, though it was more-or-less on the city's outskirts. I'm proud to say I've never run screaming to a sales event, but the fact that they existed was, and is, of course, inescapable. I was expecting mayhem. But good grief! Upon arriving, the store was predictably teeming with the masses. The store was not to open for several hours, but the groaning, grimacing ,and shoving had already ensued in full, as shoppers jockeyed for position at the front of the line. At the entrance, someone yanked my coat: "Where are *you* going?!" Umm—to *work*?! Inside, temps were milling about, surveying colossal pallets of plastic-wrapped products, chatting, looking out the windows, and chuckling, but they were visibly shaken and annoyed. I was instructed to lock fingers with other guards around one of the pallets, a tower of disposable cameras, which alone, was sufficiently hideous. The crowd surged forward, howling and crashing against the doors. When they finally swung open, the people avalanched in, and without delay, a frenzy of running, grabbing, and hollering was underway. They swarmed on the cameras, sweeping up piles of them, snatching them, and slapping them out of each other's hands, while snagging each other's coats and shirts, and bellowing at and threatening one another, as arguments erupted into fistfights. Unable to hold the line against the crush of people, guards were knocked backward onto the pallet, spilling cameras all over the floor. Everywhere people scrambled about, laughing maniacally, falling, flailing, pushing, shrieking, and throwing blows.

At the time, I was on a big online documentary kick, and I'd already watched the first installment of the Zeitgeist series, 'Human Resources,' and Adam Curtis's 'Century of the Self' and 'The Power of Nightmares.' All these films dealt with capitalism, behaviorist psychological social control, and suppressed history, and as my WalMart experience showed, they weren't exaggerating. In a way, I'd been tracking a collective nightmare, against my will, since white attacks on black elementary students in 1974 Boston. And all this capitalist commotion could theoretically, at least in part, be traced back to Bush's utterances about shopping to combat terrorism. But finding myself physically at risk, amidst an engineered mass-hysteria event, and knowing who'd conceived it, how, and why (thanks Edward Bernays) was simultaneously a new personal low and extremely illuminating. If the programmed annihilation of sanity, composure, and personal accountability weren't tragic enough, I also realized that I'd exposed myself to it out of insolvency, after being made redundant as a worker. Every temporary employee on the floor of WalMart for 'Black Friday' was a casualty. From top to bottom, the thing was an unmitigated fiasco.

Siddhartha's analysis of suffering, ignorance, clinging, craving, and the primacy of experience once again rang true. It stood up to scrutiny every time, without fail. Thus, I trust his prescription, which involves compassion; well, I do now, or more than I did in 2008 anyway. People's ignorance causes their misery and misfortune; furthermore, they are seemingly incapable of doing anything about it, or even understanding it. They're against choking the oceans with metric tons of plastic filth, but they sweep it off the shelves when it's offered in a sale. They want clean skies, but refuse to give up their oversized vehicles. And in spite of the 'fact' that 'there are 280 channels, but nothing on,' untold millions are glued to their television night after imminently predictable night. People are comfortable with pained mediocrity, and hence, far more prepared *for* change from without, than *to* change within. And then, having outsourced all agency to faceless, soulless institutions, they wonder why things only get worse. Choices have consequences. Lifestyles create policies. *We need to come to our senses.*

2009

Well you tell us it's working, that it's worth the expense
And the goal is protection, assistance, defense
The Iraqis are free
With a democracy
That functions to a greater or a lesser degree
They just need some more time, attention, and care
This war is eternal, but we're half the way there
We're fighting for freedom: we must persevere
Our enemies and our allies, are explicitly clear
But the mothers are screaming as they search for their sons
And the men shake their fists as they brandish their guns
They curse what we say, and they curse what we do
And some of it's made up, but a lot of it's true
They answer with bombs, with swords and attacks
With eye-for-eye justice, with treacherous acts
It's twisted and it's burning, it's out of control
Their priceless antiquities, looted and stole
Just living's a toil, and nobody's loyal
And the one building standing is the Ministry of Oil
Since most of the soldiers with honor have served
Some mode of respect I believe is deserved
But instead, they go digging for the armor they need
And the ceiling's collapsing when they reach Walter-Reed
Their bodies are broken, they're wounded and burned

And if they're not dead they just might be returned
They're tortured by nightmares, with pain and with guilt
For the deeds that they've done, and the blood they've spillt
They find themselves homeless, with doubt and regret
With families in trouble, with mountains of debt
So the words in your speeches don't reflect what is real
What goes on in your minds, and the way that you feel
Well you tell us it's working, that it's worth the expense
We've endured a few pitfalls, unexpected events
But here's my conclusion, from the place where I stand
Everything's going exactly as planned
To bankrupt the country, in spirit and coin
Either shut up and fuck off, or sign up and join
And accept the collapse of the nation's ideals
The monarch decrees, the plebian kneels
Can the government act without cause or restraint?
Are the people too spineless to lodge a complaint?
Could it be that they're selfish, they're tired and harassed?
All they want is a bargain for a gallon of gas?
I think it's disgusting, by now you know why
You would do well to remember, we all have to die
When it's over, my soul will ascend to the sky
And if there is hell below, may forever you fry . . .

This verse, no big surprise, was conceived as a final swing on the outgoing Bush regime, which had left the country morally and financially exhausted. Others and I noted that, yet again, a white man had made a complete mess of things, and a black man was charged with cleaning up. Obama: 'Janitor-in-Chief'? Probably too harsh, but you get my point.

By this time, I'd been laid off from the dysfunctional organization I had been working for, after the general manager absconded with over half a million dollars of its revenue. I decided to use my unemployment insurance to support myself for a year, while I articulated a new philosophy and musical genre. 2009 was an ambitious year!

The song starting this chapter was titled 'Masters of War Redux,' from my third solo album, 'Off The Grid,' and it was supposedly an update of Bob Dylan's iconic 1963 antiwar polemic, 'Masters of War;' although, I just realized that I've never gotten anyone to listen to it to the end. The album was in a style I was calling 'post Hip Hop'—i.e. devotional music with an urban edge, or Hip Hop for grown folks, which exchanged beats for an acoustic guitar. What would rap sound like with an indoor voice and a bit of travel under its belt? With this new genre, we'd find out. I was aware of at least two other emcees, Lauryn Hill and Wyclef Jean, who had made a similar transition, interestingly, both from the same group, 'The Fugees.' Maybe I could convince them to take up the 'post Hip Hop banner' and help push the genre forward. I was thinking big! Or trying to, anyway.

Besides the album, my other project was a philosophical treatise called 'The Dharma of Alternate Realism.' I envisioned it as a counternarrative to the degenerate neoconservatism of the decade, a complimentary worldview for a presumably progressive incoming administration. Since it's just about the most accurate representation of my thought at the time, I have reproduced a short sample of it here. Please recall that this was 2009.

ALTERNATE REALISM, DEFINED

Alternate: to occur in successive turns; to pass back and forth from one state, action, or place to another; to cause to follow in turns; to interchange regularly.

Realism: an inclination toward literal truth; representation in art and literature of objects, actions, or social conditions as they really are, without idealization.

It appears to have fallen out of fashion to typify world history as proceeding in an orderly, linear manner. Tidy and convenient grand unifying themes implying a kind of invisible agency moving through human endeavor are often looked at as too pat, reductionist, fanciful, superstitious. But I want to examine a particular era in world history whose general themes, whose occurrence in the first place, underscores what I feel is a central tenet to alternate realism, namely that:

Worldviews, as an aggregate of what is broadly perceived to be the literal truth can, indeed must, pass regularly from one state to another.

The period I'd like to discuss is the one commonly referred to as the Classical Age. I'm particularly interested in a roughly 100 year span, from about 550 BCE to 450 BCE.

During this relatively short time the world saw a tremendous outpouring of contemplative thought on the nature of material reality, resulting in influential philosophies, methods of discourse, new sciences, metaphysical texts and two religions. Whether or not these events were the result of an invisible agency intervening in human affairs is, of course, open to conjecture and debate. What is more certain is that the Classical Age constitutes a point of demarcation in our collective consciousness; where, for a combination of reasons, some known some not, the world would be changed forever afterward.

SUMMARY

500 BCE: the fundamentals of classical realism: rationality, observation, cause and effect, liberation from ignorance and suffering, existence of an unchanging, invisible reality from which everything emanates and which can be accessed and harnessed, are expressed in the West by the Greeks and in the East by Siddhartha Gautama, the Buddha.

The Enlightenment: a radical realignment of the physical, rational and moral universe occurs. In the center of the maelstrom are iconoclasts like Francis Bacon, Rene Descartes and Isaac Newton. Together they break with the traditions of classical realism, laying the foundations for modern science, governance and philosophy, but also relativism and the disappearance of universal objective truths.

Subjectivist Rebellion: all bets being off, a host of new philosophical strains—some actively hostile toward classical realism—are elaborated. The inclination to reach for absolutes is washed away by reductionism, separation into parts and subjugation of the natural world in order to bring about power and instruments of convenience and comfort. When every man is vested with the ultimate authority to assemble his own universe; moral or not, many choose savagery, exploitation, conquest and genocide. Universal Truth (God) is killed.

Theosophical Society: A relatively small group of mystically inclined intellects seeks to reassert the classical realist wisdom traditions: objective truth, an unchanging, invisible reality, and methods by which to alleviate suffering and bring about harmony and brotherhood on earth. Though some of their ideology is tainted by the racist, imperialist notions of the day, their efforts set the stage for an all-encompassing human potential movement. The term 'New Age' emerges for the first time in this context.

World War I and Dadaism: Inevitably, the urge to mechanized power and dominance leads to an imperialist conflagration no part of the world escapes. Another small band sees the mindless devastation as resulting directly from materialistically acquisitive values and disappearance of universal truth and a moral universe. Scattered diffusely across the globe, they begin to produce art and other cultural works whose aim is to undercut, to subvert the dominant paradigm of rationalized elitism, conquest and brutality.

Freud, Psychology, Jung and Bernays: Employing the scientific method, psychologist Sigmund Freud discovers repressed sexual urges resulting from birth and infancy are responsible for creating an unconscious which influences speech, thought and behavior. Out of these revelations emerges the discipline of psychoanalysis. Since the dominant worldview is devoid of any inherent morality the new science can be used for good or ill. Carl Jung shows that myth and magic exist in the unconscious as well, that working with the persona and the shadow can have healing effects. Ed Bernays exploits people's deepest, darkest unexpressed fears and repressed fantasies in the name of returning astronomical profit to corporations. The individualist/ consumption/ relativist orientation begins in earnest.

Surrealism: Freud's psychoanalytical methods are fused on to Dadaism, with Hegelian and Marxist dialectics, idiosyncrasy and other stuff thrown in for good measure by dissident artists and intellectuals in Paris. They seek to reveal the contents of the unconscious by experimenting with automatic, un-rationalized production of cultural artifacts. Unlike their predecessors the Dadaists however, they hope to reunite segregated elements of consciousness, bringing about reconciliation and harmony.

Postmodernism: World War II (and particularly the Bomb which vaporized Hiroshima and Nagasaki) causes the general population to become very wary and skeptical of anything claiming to be ultimate truth... or really any kind of truth at all. Postmodernism essentially predicts its own failure and obsolescence due to the fact that nothing, anywhere, at any time, can ever be certain—including postmodernism itself as a characterization. Ironically, the search for ultimate truth is reborn again, just on a deeply personal basis. Many different avenues to the truth are elaborated and experimented with.

Earth Day, 1970: Environmentalism emerges on the international scene, together with the notion that it is up to each and every one of us to safeguard the health of the only planet we know can sustain life. Seeing the earth as it really is; small, fragile, precariously beautiful against a backdrop of vast cosmic darkness, helps enormously to underscore the point that our collective fate is inextricably interwoven. Objective truth, thus expressed, claims a subtle but unmistakable victory.

New Age: Many pioneers and visionary thinkers working in all kinds of alternative disciplines produce a collective body of work so massive and varied that it defies any other description than the one it gets. From its codification as a mass media phenomenon, significant portions of it are mainstreamed into consumer culture. Because 'New Age' is increasingly associated with products and marketing, a backlash against the term emerges, detectable even on the streets of the ultra-progressive Bay Area. And yet there is a pressing need to be able to identify the various strains of the New Age movement with a term that concisely summarizes them.

Well! I never said it was my *best* writing. I included this selection to show the degree to which I was trying to express and integrate what I'd learned to that point. And some of these concepts will return, with interesting new twists, in later chapters.

Anyway, that is where I was in 2009. Again, I put my music before the music industry censors at TAXI. And again they informed me that as much as they loved the content, *I'd never sell it.* I lost a sense that I was musically relevant.

The world had moved on. Maybe *I* ought to. Later that year, a video of the Subterraneanz randomly surfaced on Youtube, featuring a song from the *Subterranean Means* album called "Sleep N' Beauty." Six years after the band had imploded, people—not exactly hordes—began coming forward in the comments section about how much they'd loved the band 'back in the day.' I didn't know how to take it. Was I . . . 'that dude?' 'Old Rap Nigga?'

2011

Orpheus traveled through Hades
In pursuit of his wife Eurydice
Not seeking initiation into a mystery
He only wanted her back, matter of fact
After she fell through a crack
In the planet, due to a snakebite attack
Sang a song so sad he made the gods cry
They pointed a way—told him you can beat the odds by
Leading her out, not looking back, just going forth in trust
If you fail, she forever bites the dust—it's not up to us
He found her though she was a shadow
His heart leapt, they crept
to the gate where the border between the worlds is kept
The sun poured in at the portal
He couldn't resist, looked in her face
And she became immortal
Some speculate the whole thing was a trick
It was the gods fucking around, just being a dick
Egyptian Book of the Dead, Ishtar, Gilgamesh
Set out to fulfill a quest to kill the flesh
To merge into the Cosmic mesh
Jesus was led into the desert by the Holy Spirit
To confront the devil; to see, hear it, and not fear it
Krishna visited the Lord of Death, Yama, to defeat karma

Sometimes I wonder about Barack Obama . . .
It's like we're all initiates in a mystery school
This is why history's cool
Mythological archetypes penetrate
The false veil of space and time
And land in your man's rhyme
Did we get a High Priest, a Trickster, or a Sacrificial Lamb?
Damn! I am
Only tryna put y'all's mind on a different program
So you bound by no man
While we navigatin' No Man's Land
Nyambezi, the Black Bodhisattva
From the Pleiadian Star system
Blessing y'all with platinum-bar wisdom
Let me take you down, cause we're going to
Not Strawberry Fields, up with your shields
While we journey through the Underworld . . .

By 2011, I was feeling pretty goddamn sure—regardless of the black president—that we were living through 'Hell on Earth.' I vaguely remember reading that Old Sid, the Tathagata himself (i.e. the Buddha), had said something similar; and as bleak as 'Hell on Earth' sounds, it makes all the sense in the world that he would have said it, given the apocalyptic chaos plaguing his time.

I was now transitioning from a deep ecology framework, to a framework of deep-time. It took me weeks to reach the point where I could write about what was going on, and I still shudder so deeply thinking about it that I will only briefly touch upon the subject. Better yet, here's another segment of lyrics, like the above, from my song *Journey Through the Underworld*, which summarizes what I was witnessing:

Pachamama bring drama, and who could blame her
We overreached like a muthafucka
When we tried to tame her
Too much dynamiting, too much blighting
Too much fighting
Too much buildin', too much drillin', too much killin'
Too much disregard for the children
Too much waste dischargin', too much garbage and
Too many disenfranchised living at the margin
Too many dancing with the devil in a fool's bargain—
It's not jargon
Ever wonder why birds dropping out of the sky?
Or these fishkills be ill, piling up yay high?
Baby dolphins washing up on the shore, I can assure
That that Gulf crude oil gusher was more than a metaphor
We penetrated clear through to Hell without a backup plan
What you expect to come back up, man?
Supercells and storm swells rearrange the coastline
Tsunamis are caused by earthquakes most times
The black smoke lets you know that there's a situation
And now the region's being cleared for fear of radiation . . .
We have the dubious distinction
Of being the first species to cause mass extinction
I'm telling y'all, there's a war in our collective psyche
Resulting in exactly what be on the news nightly . . .

Clearly though, I wasn't the only one to have figured this out. Also making a regular appearance in the nightly news that year was a little number called 'the Occupy Movement'—in essence, late-1960s-style socio-political agitation reloaded for a digital millennium. Beginning very appropriately in a park across from Wall Street in New York City, Occupy metastasized rapidly via digital technology into a global phenomenon, sparking protests in nearly a thousand cities across the planet. One of them, naturally, was Oakland. One day, after continually hearing a din of police sirens, helicopters, and breathless reports of 'eyesore,' makeshift camps on the green of City Hall, I decided to check it out. It *was* shocking to have the scene at 14th and Broadway come into view. The concourse had indeed been turned into a gigantic squatter's camp. Throngs of activists had converged on the downtown area with signs, banners, readied cameras and phones, bullhorns, and drums. Police were posted around the perimeter looking tense, having been roundly criticized for heavy-handed tactics against protesters and the many homeless who were among them. Bands of black-clad anarchists were milling about, chatting, pontificating, taunting police, and politicking, sometimes testily, with groups of young blacks, passersby on bicycles, mohawked punks, and people wearing ponchos, fisherman hats, and tie-dyed t-shirts. Well! THIS was *interesting*!

Magnetized by the melee, I drifted into the encampment, and quickly discovered that though it sprawled and appeared shambly, with its tents, tarps, plaster, cardboard, corrugated metal shelters, and pallet walkways on saturated, muddy grass, it was surprisingly organized and digitally outfitted. Everywhere people were on laptops and phones—filming, texting, blogging, and podcasting away.

Upon closer inspection, the encampment was doing much more than simply critiquing and protesting capitalism; they were actively remedying it by providing free food, shelter, and medical care. Basic needs were being met. They had bicycle-powered appliances (free energy), a children's center, and an improvised research library, for example.

Occupy Wall Street had inspired the 'Battle of Oakland,' a series of high-profile occupations beginning in October, 2011. After enacting a General Assembly in support of Indigenous Rights, activists set up camp on Frank Ogawa Plaza at City Hall, renaming it Oscar Grant Plaza, after the young brother slain by a BART transit cop in 2009. This began the collaborative erection of several protest encampments across the city, followed unfailingly by extreme reactions from law enforcement. It was assumed that the administration of former progressive activist-turned-mayor Jean Quan would be sympathetic and accommodating to demonstrator activities. Instead, she, apparently, repeatedly authorized police to unload fusillades of high-velocity bean bags, rubber bullets, percussion grenades, smoke bombs, and tear gas against the protestors, which nearly killed former Marine and Iraq War veteran Scott Olsen. But as the slogan went: *When Oakland is under attack—what do we do? Stand Up, Fight Back!* Once again, this defiant stance was widely understood to be a legacy of the bold radicalism of late 1960s Black Panthers. Before it was all said and done, Occupy protesters organized a general strike, which effectively shut down the Port of Oakland. It's important to recall that this victory was situated within a broader justice movement, which included the Arab Spring, uprisings in Spain, Portugal, Iceland, Greece, and elsewhere. Still very much influenced by Marxism, the movement's complex economic narrative was distilled into a pithy statement about a tiny, entrenched, global, ultra-elite called the '1 percent,' and the rest of us, a long-suffering, viciously exploited '99 percent.' It was a masterstroke. The elegant simplicity and accuracy of *"We are the 99 percent!"* permitted even children to thoughtfully participate, as they did during the march on the Port of Oakland.

What's so crazy—and it only dawned on me *how* crazy hours before writing this—is that at the time, thanks to president Obama's tuition-debt renegotiation program, I found myself returning to college as a middle-aged man in the midst of the most significant social revolt in decades. Amplifying that craziness was the fact that the decision to go back to school was as much basic survival strategy, as desire for self-improvement. Bottom line, I needed money. It was increasingly clear that as I was corporations had no use for me. The feeling was mutual. Criminality was a non-starter, since I had zero qualifications whatsoever. I had a little bit of nothing to sell, and although my eyesight was slowly getting poorer, it wasn't poor enough to qualify for SSI disability benefits. Consequently, I was chronically behind on rent. So there I was in 2011, a forty-two-year-old former rapper, spending the lion's share of my financial aid on enrollment in the Peralta college system—Berkeley City, Laney, and Alameda—and paying what was left over to my landlord. After working out how much I needed to spend on school supplies, household items, communication, and transportation, I was lucky if I could scrape together enough spare change for a breakfast sandwich. Yay, Capitalism.

If you're willing and positioned to ruthlessly exploit, despoil, lie, cheat, and steal—behavior that would get you institutionalized in a saner society—or are related to someone thus positioned, then the system is 'all to da' good.' For anyone and everyone else, sentient beings on the planet, and the planet *itself*, the system is Hell—point blank. Furthermore, illusion-shattering anecdotes were beginning to leak out, exposing that life for the so-called 'winners,' the one percent, wasn't necessarily anything to shout from the rooftops about. These anecdotes shattered the public's perception, since the only information the general public was once allowed on the subject were variations of 'Lifestyles of the Rich and Famous.' In order to preserve *tha Game*, the supposed inevitable superiority of free-market economics, the masses were strictly prohibited from seeing the dysfunction, drug abuse, sexual deviancy, and mental degeneracy of the individuals presumed to be our intellectual and moral betters. And this is not just me talking out my ass either. Books like Dr. Paul Babiak and Dr. Robert Hare's *Snakes in Suits: When Psychopaths Go To Work*, and the entertainingly devastating documentary *I Am Fish Head*, attested that we'd all been profoundly and catastrophically duped about human nature, economics, and the true requirements for happiness. I'd already read Daniel Gilbert's *Stumbling on Happiness*, and Barbara Ehrenreich's *Bright Sided: How Positive Thinking Undermines America*. I was really coming to grips with the depths of the deception, how truly fucked-over we'd all been. And I clearly recognized that the money I was borrowing for education, though a necessary and temporary stopgap, was, in the long run, only more firmly ensnaring me in the debt-economy system.

What could I do? Just by being born, I was compelled to journey through the underworld, through Hell, suffering with all sentient beings. My karmic assignment of 'black' and 'male,' in a world designed by and for white men, was only one layer of it, though a powerful, decisive one. Whether or not I *caused* the problem had no bearing whatsoever on the situation. Siddhartha's astute analysis, time and again, proved unshakable.

I had to do *something*. I couldn't hurl myself into Occupy though—my first semester was starting! In a small storefront, at the dustier edge of downtown Oakland, there was an intriguing operation I'd heard about, called the East Bay Meditation Center. Urban Buddhism! *Now* we were getting somewhere. From my first visit, surrounded by Black, White, Asian, Latino, young, old, LGBT, and differently-abled disciples of 'the Blessed One,' I felt a distinct and refreshing sense of authentic community, that I hadn't experienced since the days of the Subterraneanz. And this one was aware, the way I was. The way EBMC organized sits and other activities on different nights, to accommodate the needs of separate groups and the community-at-large, seemed to be an eloquent way of taking things on 'as they really are,' with compassion and skillful means. With sirens blaring away outside, people would share the impact the Dharma was making on their lives, their personal and group struggles within society, and the many different, yet interrelated, ways they had been marginalized and traumatized. Revealingly, this included anecdotes about the marginalization of whites in the very diverse Bay Area milieu. And they weren't content with merely sitting on their mats either. At some point, they began holding training sessions in Kingian nonviolent resistance, adapting it to address unique challenges, such as maintaining an upright, dignified sitting posture while blocking an entrance in protest, or facing down police. It was a start! I felt energized and inspired by them.

If I didn't have essays to turn in, readings, and jazz ensemble rehearsals, I may very well have participated in EBMC's support of Occupy. But it just so happened that I had a Beginning Film and Video class, at Laney in Oakland, with local celebrity and host of the *Days With Zahrah* travel program Zahrah Farmer. When she instructed the class to come up with video projects, what sprang, nearly fully-formed, from my mind was a documentary titled *You Are Your Own Guru*. Of course! Now I could make an artifact fixed in a medium, a tangible expression of my worldview and philosophy that would be accessible, entertaining, and enlivening. But to build a documentary on your own, even a short one, from scratch, with other subjects to study and severely limited time and resources, was no punk; we only had one semester, and the whole class had to learn about and share cameras, microphones, etc. I quietly beseeched the Tirthankaras (who, according to Jainism, are beings that have formed a passage for other sentient beings to cross over the endless stream of rebirths), to make Zahrah let me do the project on my own. Um . . . yeah, NO. She assigned to me a 'crew' of fellow students—one which was not particularly sympathetic to, or even remotely familiar with, anything I was talking about. In fact—how to put this generously—most of the time, especially in the beginning, I oscillated wildly between amused disbelief and homicidal rage over certain characters actively sabotaging my efforts. More than once, my Dharma game (wisdom, compassion, skillful means) was pushed to the limits, as people around me goofed off, laughing and jabbering with each other, while I was trying to stage a scene.

Gradually, one of them, a young sister named Latajh, decided to take the project seriously, and that began to move things swiftly forward. Still, we had to navigate scheduling interviews, equipment malfunctions, and learning and using Final Cut Pro—yikes! But we got it done; and when we showed our final product, I was startled and heartened by the way fellow students, including 'resigned' members of my so-called crew, suddenly understood and resonated with the film's message. Mind you, this was an Oakland community college with a local population, whom I was not exactly encountering during my New Age encounter-group days. Yet there I was, beside myself with exuberant hope for the future, as students excitedly talked about the Law of Attraction, and gave moving personal anecdotes about 'how the universe worked' in their lives.

During the editing of *You Are Your Own Guru*, I tried to incorporate footage I'd made of Occupy. Walking carefully across boards, with expensive equipment, in Oscar Grant Plaza, accompanied by my trusty co-producer Latajh, I'd figured surely *someone* there would be able to give me thoughtful, or at least usable, soundbites on the intersection of inner, spiritual work and outer, political activism. *E-yeah, no.* As it turned out, the idea was a much tougher sell than I'd imagined. Fortunately, I was able to tap into the wisdom of longtime social activist, bestselling author, publisher of Tikkun Magazine, leader of the Network of Spiritual Progressives, and my friend, Rabbi Michael Lerner, who gave a beautiful, clear, comprehensive, practical, and rousing rendition of the idea, in what he calls a 'New Bottom Line' for America. It more or less saved the documentary's central point—that contemplation of deeper meaning, engagement with an invisible, but real, inner world, mindful kindness, and generosity were not only personal concerns, but *absolutely vital* to establish in the domain of human affairs, if we are to continue on a precariously damaged and finite planet. Although I didn't capture them on film, there were powerful moments I witnessed during Occupy where these principles did indeed come into view; even if I had gotten the shots, I couldn't have fit them into a 12 minute documentary, but they nevertheless expressed the essence of the thing. At one juncture, a cadre of First Nations people—whose presence at Occupy, from the jump, reliably lent spiritual gravitas to the situation—decided that their voices were not cutting through the noise; well-meaning, resource-rich, white liberals were *again* coopting and colonizing the movement. I attended an afternoon breakaway plebiscite, where they united with other marginalized groups and decided to disrupt the General Assembly that was to take place later on that evening; and that's exactly what they did. Not long after the first checks of the 'People's Mic,' the coalition seized the floor, and began to articulate a long list of racist and classist betrayals of Occupy by white activists. The response to this? Silence. But deeper—tapping. As I looked around, I noticed dozens of white faces in the crowd of hundreds, with blue tints cast upon them as they solemnly hovered over laptops and tablets. In the cold dark of the large outdoor amphitheater, they were furiously typing, recording as much of the coalition's grievances as could be captured. Realizing this information would eventually make it into blogs, podcasts, and other social media outlets covering the movement, I found myself feeling *some kind of way.* Technology was being used for a genuine, respectful, self-reflective effort to thoroughly analyze and confront the many wrongs of the past (for a change); maybe this really was 'what democracy looks like' in 2011. Wiping my eyes, I turned on my heels and walked home, thinking "huh . . . *we might just pull it off . . .*"

P.S. Last time I checked, the documentary was still available on Youtube. You can see it for yourself if you search "You Are Your Own Guru," and keep scrolling down, until you see a blue-tinted, Cinemascope-ish thumbnail of a guy looking like a Rabbi (that would indeed be Rabbi Michael Lerner). Sadly, or appropriately, depending on one's viewpoint, only one shot of Occupy made the final cut: a flyer, taped to the window of EBMC's storefront office, depicting a body seated in the lotus position, captioned: *OCCUPY THE PRESENT—DIG DEEP, POWER UP.*

2012

Now let's proceed to eschatology, vindicating teleology
Philosophy, merging with religiosity
With a healthy dose of ancient astronomy
That predicts the imminent collapse
Of the planet's sustaining ecology
You've seen the movies, or at least the ads
Geological upheavals—that make heroes
Out of suburban dads
Certain fads like cataclysm have cache in culture
A sadder vision that alas may have some realism
The King Wen sequence of the I Ching
Made Dennis McKenna conclude
That Mayan priests said the right thing
He called it Time Wave Zero—might be a guy thing
Like Zeus up in the Heavens trying
To be frightening with lightning
The theory states novelty reiterates
In chaos that creates complexity, marked by dates
At the beginnings and ends of epochs
That get shorter and shorter
Eventually inducing a New Order;
Teilhard De Chardin was convinced
Humankind was evolving to a fusion with God, ever since
We went on two feet... of course, Christian literalists believe

That we're all doomed for the transgressions of Eve
The common factor is convergence
Leading to emergence of some sort of final outcome
Hence the urgency
They and we, feel and see
Trying to predict what the hell 2012 is gonna be;
If Chardin is right, we all go home—wow
If McKenna is right, it all collapses into Now
If Christians are right, a tiny few are raptured
Leaving the rest of us heathens for the devil to capture:
Now I'm not sure, any more than anyone else
But I have my ideas, which I'm happy to share, if you care
I'm here for my peers, not myself
In other words, y'all come first
But I'm out of bars, you'll have to wait till the next verse . . .

To paraphrase the chorus of the above song: this was my intellectual Tai Chi, highly accomplished, you didn't want to take it lightly. Like other strange synchronicities in my life, it's fitting that I'm covering this material on Christmas Day of 2017. The 'end of the world' scenarios I'm referring to in the above rhyme were presumed to be scheduled for December 21st, 2012, the day of the Winter Solstice. This subject constitutes another whole potential range of especially unhinged ramblings and rantings. But to stay on task and deal with personal and collective schizophrenia, hybridity, evolution, and the Buddha Dharma, I should probably make some very basic points about deep-time for the sake of context.

At this moment in the human saga, we track time based on something called 'the Gregorian Calendar,' established in the late 16th century by Pope Gregory XIII, as an update of the much older Julian Calendar, proposed, perhaps not shockingly, by Julius Caesar, during the heyday of the Roman Empire ('empire' being the operative word to consider here). The Roman Empire used the calendar to synchronize the timing of civil and liturgical affairs; from an Afrocentric point of view, this synchronization could be characterized as a consolidation of white male supremacy, across domains of human activity — economics, education, entertainment, labor, law, politics, religion, sex, and war — as an act of coercive control over the reality of its subjects, many of whom were Africans with spiritual traditions of *deep*, i.e. more authoritative, antiquity. The many Christian ecumenical councils were a part of this consolidation process, as the Church attempted to reach canonical consensus about issues such as sin, redemption, key Biblical events, the nature of Jesus, etc; the oft-cited Nicaean Creed was the result of the first of these councils. There are however other calendars, or interpretations of time, linked to different cultural/spiritual systems, particularly older ones based on untold periods of observation and record-keeping, which might provide more meaningful measurement and predictive efficacy. Some scholars would argue that the calendar we use now has its ultimate origins in 'Babylonian time.' Poetic enough, but there are still other calendars that might be considered, such as the 'Egyptian' or 'Mayan'. A society is a reflection of the time it keeps (in case you were wondering why the world looks the way it does today). Instead of a Romanized, linear, left-brained, mechanistic interpretation of earthly events, calendars like the Egyptian and Mayan propose a *cyclical* rising and falling of civilizations, based on earthly correspondence with celestial alignments ('as above, so below'). If time was seen as cyclical, and not linear, Roman dominance could be perceived as temporary and vulnerable, rather than logically fixed, inevitable, and inherently better. Some alternate calendars acknowledge a highly mysterious phenomenon inherent in the solar system, called 'the Precession of the Equinoxes,' which involves celestial observation occurring over a vast span of time, approximately twenty-five thousand years. In addition to the Earth's daily spin and yearly journey around the Sun, there is a subtle wobble of the planet on an invisible fixed axis in space, which causes different constellations to be visible in the night sky at any given point. These constellations, described in and as the Zodiac signs, portend radical shifts in earthly energies and events as the heavenly bodies change position. Therefore, sagas of human history can be characterized as 'ages.' The 'Great Year' of the classical Greeks, or the '*yugas*' of Hindu philosophy, also speak of vast spans of time in which organizational paradigms and their associated civilizations routinely rise and fall.

For more detailed information about all this: gravitation, magnetism, angular momentum, heliacal risings, polar stars, companion stars, ancient observatories/ritualistic sites, and the like, I'd suggest the absurdly elegant documentary, available on Youtube, called 'The Great Year,' which breaks down the Precession, apparently validated by modern astronomical observation.

One cosmology proclaiming the Precession of the Equinoxes as its time-reference base is the Mayan creation narrative, recounted in Mesoamerican sacred texts, such as the *Popol Vuh*, and the *Chilam Balam*. To track much longer cycles, the Mayans engineered a complex 'Long Count calendar;' many will be familiar with the sunstone image covered with strange glyphs and a face at the center of its visual depiction.

New Age artist, author, founder of the Earth Day Festival, and coordinator of the 1987 Harmonic Convergence, Jose Arguelles, issued a 'Law of Time' based on a vivid synthesis of the Mayan creation narrative, chakras and Tantra, the I Ching, Pythagorean mathematics, the Seven Heavens of Islam, Jungian analytic psychology, ancient astronaut theory (i.e. extraterrestrials), and beyond. Now, Arguelles's teachings describe a cosmological order of immense proportion, featuring highly arcane, nearly inscrutable terms like Baktun, Katun, the Galactic Core (or Hunab-Ku), the AA Relay Station, Central Stellar Radeon, psi-banks, activation portals, universal resonant holons, alpha-beta zones, telepathic structures, holo-mind perceivers, megacarpins, myriads, field compressors, absolute radial codons, radial hyper-plasmas, Maori tubes, and many more. Some of these terms I grok, others not so much, and interestingly enough, a few of them describe phenomena I've had direct personal experience with (more on that later). To try and explain as simply as possible why I'm droning on about this: Arguelles's theory, in essence, was that an intelligent invisible matrix called the noosphere surrounds Earth, holographically projecting what we experience as 'consensus reality' from extradimensional superstructures in progressively remoter corners of the Universe. Babylonian time, which has marked the last Long Count, an age that has been disastrous for the planet, was expected to end at the close of the 12th Baktun, on December 21, 2012. After that, mathematically encoded extradimensional information will be increasingly downloaded through the cosmic holographic system to Earth, causing a deep-time epochal shift from a severely degraded age to a more evolved one. The information being projected into the hologram includes telepathic and other extrasensory capacities (available at first only to those who can perceive and cultivate them), imprinted with creational energy-infused numerical codes programmed to trigger the emergence of an idealized archetypal superconscious Earth civilization. Beginning with a relatively small cadre of adepts in the evolved paradigm, humans will gradually be psycho-spiritually equipped and induced to transmute and transcend the suffering of the entire sentient planet.

If that all sounds unnecessarily verbose and contorted, what I'm talking about here is your basic 'dawning of the Age of Aquarius,' rather beautifully summarized in the Fifth Dimension's late 60s hit song by that name—"Mystic crystal revelation/the mind's true liberation, Aquarius!" How many music fans recognized these lyrics as an expression of a deep-time cyclical prophecy perhaps hundreds of thousands of years in the making? I don't know. What I can say for sure is that the Mayan Long Count meta-narrative I just described was a significant component of the highly infectious mythical hype surrounding the approach of December 21, 2012.

Arguelles's thought, like that of Terence (not Dennis, as I mistakenly said in the rhyme) McKenna, was influenced powerfully by Jesuit philosopher-priest Pierre Teilhard de Chardin, whose ideas about evolution as a divinely orchestrated planetary reunion with God had an outsized impact on the New Age movement. 2012 theory enthusiast and poetic polymath Terence McKenna, reportedly at the behest of the many psychoactive plants he ingested, went several steps further, asserting that the emergence of novelty and complexity in nature (including human nature) would accelerate to a point, where the past, present, and future, everything that was, is, or could ever possibly be, would be fully manifest in one ongoing, unfathomably intense hyper-eternal NOW.

These titillating and relatively hopeful musings on the year's outcomes, however, were not without their considerably darker counterpart. It could be argued that the mythical hype over 2012 was in fact 50% New Age driven, and 50% the product of Christian fundamentalists with a literal interpretation of the New Testament. Unlike their New Age soothsaying cousins, Christian literalists were adamant that the date would mean God's justly, wrathful ending of a world hopelessly corrupted by Original Sin—that would, of course, be Revelation, the Four Horsemen, the final war of Armageddon (not at all a love and light affair of global super consciousness). And since 'if it bleeds, it leads,' popular culture, primed by tales of zombies and attacks from space, latched much more vigorously onto 2012 as actual apocalypse.

Major news publications like TIME Magazine took note of the fact that there was already a healthy cottage industry of plays, movies, books, comics, and television shows portraying fantastical, civilization-vaporizing catastrophe way before the runup to the dreaded date of December 21. Networks like the History and the Discovery Channel poured gasoline on the rising flames of Final Judgment with wildly speculative programs, that though hilarious to view from some comfortable seat five years *after* the fact, feverishly and terrifyingly blurred the lines between fact and fiction about how it all would go down. Well, the

Sun could have a series of violent massive coronal ejections that would knock satellites out of the sky and collapse the power grid, plunging Earth into chaotic darkness! Or, maybe the ejections would weaken our atmospheric protections and the planet would be fried by solar radiation! Or, it could be that the ejections activate molten energies underground, triggering picturesque earthquakes, mega-volcanoes, and tsunamis that scour the coastlines! Or, they might scramble the Earth's magnetic polarity so badly that the surface crust actually slides out of its current position, rearranging whole continents. Okay, maybe not, BUT . . . a weakened magnetosphere *could* end photosynthesis, destroying the food chain! Matter of fact, what if the problem wasn't Earth or the Sun, but an undetected rogue planet hurtling into the Solar system from some ungodly quadrant of the cosmos on a life-annihilating collision course with Earth? Planet X (aka Nibiru) was coming!

What helped to make these exhortations especially creepy is that they were, for the most part, scientifically sound in principle. Granted, any of these scenarios would be extreme and unlikely, but they couldn't be entirely ruled out either. Between New Agers, cryptohistorian authors like Zecharia Sitchin, Erick Von Danniken, Graham Hancock, etc., Christian literalists, and Earth and space scientists all promoting alternative, or what some would call 'pseudo,' planetary chronologies, you had enough confusion and terror on deck to make a very edgy public.

As for me: I was a former rapper/activist, who'd awakened on a ten-day meditation retreat, returning to college as an adult in a time of tremendous upheaval. What can I tell you? I shared Terence McKenna's sentiment: the world could be *anything*. Or, to paraphrase British/Indian mathematician J.B.S. Haldane: 'The Universe is not only stranger than we think; it is stranger than we *can* think.' I only knew very generally about the Mayan predictions—nothing of Relay Stations and Maori Tubes—and was more a New Age, amateur, crypto-historian than Christian literalist. Yet it was clear that at some perceivable level the world as we knew it was disintegrating rapidly; after all, just in the previous year I had witnessed earthquakes, superstorms, killer tsunamis, catastrophes from crude oil and nuclear power, and massive, unexplained animal die-offs.

If I have to pinpoint any kind of position, I'd say I thought of myself as maybe 65% unconvinced of impending disaster (but more-or-less prepared for the worst, at least mentally), and 35% convinced of impending doom (but scared and not prepared). In *reality*, deep down inside, however, it was more like 55% convinced and not ready, and 45% unconvinced, but ready—if that makes any sense. It's even bamboozling for me to read it back! That's the point though: my mind was sputtering with lots of cognitive dissonance.

Had I stumbled into some verboten realm of ultra-clear seeing, that would put me at odds with the status-quo, in ways that made my youthful militancy look like child's play? Or was I simply going batshit like everyone else? Wasn't I too old for this type of shit? Spewing philosophy and presuming to launch a new genre, who exactly did I think

I was anyway? Why didn't I bite the bullet, grind my way to a proper job, find someone to settle down with like a normal middle-aged man, and get over it? The answer was simple—I couldn't. I had to do *something*, but I didn't know what. And thanks to Alan Watts, there was the Buddhist/Taoist notion of *wu-wei*, 'doing non-doing,' to consider as well. *Wu-wei* indicated being effortless, effortless being, and advanced skill in the art of getting things done, without so much as lifting a finger; but what the hell does that mean?!

In addition to 2012 possibly being the end of the world, *again* (for real, for real this time) it was also an election year. I never had any serious doubt that Obama would prevail over Romney; although, in the months preceding the election, I felt predictable twinges of nervousness watching the horse-race coverage of the polls.

Looking back over my atrocious writing from that period, I remember that California state politics and the budget were a big focus of mine. After Occupy, I was fired up with no outlet. I have documents proposing workshops to EBMC and other organizations, with names like 'Now What?' and 'Mindful Militancy,' alongside essay after essay about social ills, the Left, the New Age movement, Hip Hop, and Vipassanā. I was also fruitlessly trying to get my burgeoning book, *The Dharma of Alternate Realism*, in front of a larger audience, beyond a few students and teachers, my writers group, and shrinking cypher circle.

At some point, after participating in a lively student-march on Sacramento, I figured it was time to launch a new third political party: the Lotus Party (the lotus of course being a potent symbol of enlightenment and the Buddha). Most of my prose concerning this 'Lotus Party' is insufferable. But one slightly less obnoxious offering was the following 'notice of action':

OUR LEADERS have failed to represent our interests in even the most meager of ways. Time and time again, they cave in to wealthy financiers, lobbyists, Wall Street, bankers, hedge-fund managers, stockholders, corporate executives, and conservative brain trusts. It seems there is no limit to what they will sacrifice to fill their offshore accounts and reelection war chests. Politicians in the Beltway, as well as in the halls of state capitals, and the people who are paid fabulously to solicit their support, have entirely lost touch with the dynamics of survival in the real world, where the masses suffer dearly for political intransigence and, in some cases, scorn.

IN THE STATE OF CALIFORNIA, for example, corporations and wealthy individuals are allowed to avoid paying taxes commensurate with their income. And if the solutions to the budget crisis posed by 'Democratic' governor Jerry Brown are any indication, the state's legislators intend to furnish these people with riches at our expense. The California Budget Project has determined that in 2008 *fewer than 150,000 Californians had a total income of $208 billion*. To put the numbers into perspective: 8% of the combined total income of 1% of the state's population could completely resolve the 26 billion dollar budget deficit. This very small financial imposition would allow services and programs vital to the education, health, security, and general well-being of the citizenry to remain intact. One would think that the beneficiaries of the state's innovators would do whatever it took to preserve the state's future prospects. Instead, they appear hell-bent on wasting the very talent responsible for California's position as a world-class economy.

THEREFORE, by this document, we officially proclaim our intent to launch a student-led political party whose inception we will celebrate by organizing a statewide boycott/walk-out/strike. In the first week of May, on a date of our unanimous choosing, millions of students, teachers, administrators, parents, activists, cashiers, drivers, civil servants, web developers, artists, bakers, union members, transportation workers, restaurant owners, and others from all walks of life will refuse to perform their daily required function. Rather, they will collectively march on the state capital in Sacramento to let Jerry Brown and our legislators know, in no uncertain terms, that we will no longer stand idly by while so few are enriched on the backs of so many. If necessary, we will have a contingency plan prepared to stay in the capitol building, as did protesters in Wisconsin. We will undertake these actions under a political entity, that we will expand to leverage power against disaffected politicians, develop a People's Platform, roll out a human scale economy, as well as other activities. Wealthy Californians must pay their fair share!

. . . Except, there was no 'we'—not in the slightest. Everyone knows that an ant can't move a rubber tree plant; but I had high hopes!

As usual, my lyrics were tighter than my prose, and likely more interesting and inspiring. So here is a verse from another song I recorded that year, called *Lotus Party*, which outlines what I intended the organization to do:

We need a New Bottom Line
That doesn't revolve around 'I,' 'me,' or 'mine'
That holds the Cosmos as inherently divine
Deliberately placed before humankind
To define a positive sign
One sign is the Lotus, the symbol for purity
Transcendent wisdom, spiritual maturity
It rise through the muck; never gets stuck
Into the sunshine of joy, health, luck
Liberation, creation, what restricts it? Money!
Tiny elite get all the days that be sunny
Lavish living, rivers of milk and honey
The rest of us get the business, it's hardly funny
Democrat? Republican? Same thing

A corporate party, with a left and right wing
Nothing's ever gonna jump off until we bring
Power to bear against it—First Ring
Second Ring: what power? Universal
Declaration of Values, not commercial
A People's Platform
Bullet-pointed summary of
Common demands we hold as a norm
Third Ring: human scale economy
Local currency, regional autonomy
Neighborhood food production, 'green' construction
Holistic health, jobs, crime reduction
We consciously integrate —logic, morality
People power, kindness, spirituality
The Rings are the things the Lotus Party will do
We may even run a candidate for President too!
The first Three Rings make the Fourth Ring possible
With careful planning, unlikely becomes plausible;
Design and export this scalable system
To facilitate a mass withdrawal from globalism!

Again, the "New Bottom Line" was a declaration of progressive political policy, conceived by Rabbi Lerner and promoted by the Network of Spiritual Progressives. It looks like I was thinking of the Lotus Party as an electoral apparatus for the Network, or something to that effect; but it's not that they or anyone else encouraged me to start it.

Around this time, one of my instructors at Berkeley City College suggested I draw up a proposal for a Leadership Academy for Men of Color, which I did. It was in her communications class where I got, maybe for the first time ever, direct, specific, and spontaneous feedback about my general affect, from people other than friends, family, romantic partners, or members of encounter groups. Berkeley City College students were very much a no-nonsense demographic; they were everyday people with kids, jobs, mortgages, rent, and other bills, who were in school to gain new skills, self-improve, graduate, and keep it moving, not to 'kick it,' 'experiment,' or 'figure themselves out.' At 43, I respected and admired that, and counted myself among them, although we all understood we were mostly going our separate ways. One day, we were discussing various communication problems that exist between men and women; and finally, after anecdotes from women about an issue they had faced in communicating with men, I said frustratedly: "Hey! *I* don't do that . . ." Immediately, a lady piped up: "You're intimidating!" And for the next few instructive moments, other women testified how they found me to be 'too much' in one way or another. My problem wasn't a failure to communicate, but that I communicated something scary from jump. When a particular woman—a six-foot, dark-skinned, broad-shouldered bus driver for the City of Oakland with neck-length dreads—told me how intimidating she found me (all of 5 feet 6), I knew there was something there to consider carefully.

Actually, it was consistent with a theme to which I was only beginning to awaken. Strangers in my presence would say words like 'scary,' 'powerful,' and the like. When two women struck up a conversation with me at a pizza parlor, I asked them, puzzled, "You all sat down next to me and started talking. Are *you* scared?" "Terrified!" shouted the more talkative one, obviously a New Yorker. I wasn't intentionally setting out to be this spooky, 'Dark-Neo type,' but I was starting to feel like I was seeing vague, fleeting glimpses of such a reflection through random daily interactions. So, linking together a lot of data points, I thought, 'Maybe this instructor is right.' Being awake, powerful, compelling, and audacious enough to write philosophy, start genres, and found political parties (none of which I was particularly succeeding at), maybe I did have some sort of coaching or leadership brand to offer. Well, I tried. The Leadership Academy for Men of Color would, presumably, be a place I could put other males, mostly brothers as I envisioned it, up on my kind of game. But in shopping around yet another highly verbose, slightly irritating piece of political agitprop, I found that not only were the teachers much more activist than the students, but the teachers themselves were not going to galvanize behind anything I was trying to do. They'd tell me they supported me; they just wouldn't be involved in any way.

Ultimately, from time to time I would remember that I was caught up in this weird paranormal cycle of dissolution and falling away, which seems to follow spiritual breakthroughs. There I was with all this 'power' or whuteva, but with little else. I had all these ideas and projects to propagate, but no marketing savvy or self-promotional skill (others handled those tasks for The Exile Society/ Subterraneanz). My family band and most consequential intimate relationship were long over. I'd recorded songs, including one specifically for powerhouse Bay Area independent radio station KPFA, that I couldn't get anyone to take seriously. I was getting further and further behind on rent, and scrounging around for enough money to eat a single meal per day. My eyesight was getting poorer, family and friends were caught up in their own struggles, and to add insult to injury, this 'power' of mine was beginning to make me fidgety and paranoid. I was getting like that 80s song with Rockwell and Michael Jackson: *"I always feel like somebody's watching me . . ."*

There is another whose name I haven't mentioned yet, Ko Ko Jaeger, who heavily influenced my state and life through 2012, and I'd be remiss to not mention her. I'd met her at an Enneagram personality-typing workshop, in the early days of my post-9/11 foray into the encounter-group scene, the same event where I'd met my former ol' lady with whom I went to India. On that day, Ko Ko, in short order, magnetized my attention when her penetrating, saucer-sized eyes fixated on me, from across a fairly sexually-charged living room somewhere in the Berkeley hills. Daughter of the court astrologer for Timothy Leary's disruptive clique of LSD-soaked radical intellectuals, Ko Ko and I formed a bond of friendship with that special, eerie, immediate intimacy reserved for tales of cosmos-fated communion—think 'soul contracts' and whatnot. After discovering we had a curious amount of personality quirks in common, especially for a black guy and a white woman, we became an inseparable duo of '(Gen) X-Files.' I loved how much her droll, dark, nerdy sense of humor reminded me of mine. We were like independent inquisitors of the movement. She was right by my side for many of the excursions into the self-realization modalities I mentioned getting into after 9/11; and we often griped to each other about how politically correct and non-combative (i.e. mild) it all seemed. It was during one night of especially spirited and saucy griping—with the two of us trying to imagine a philosophy for a bolder, more reckless, cadre of truth seekers—that I spat out the term *alternate realism*. In short, there wasn't anything I couldn't, and few things I didn't, run past her for the lucid, provocative response I knew I'd get; and she never disappointed, even once. The 'rings' of the Lotus Party agenda were most likely inspired by her notion of the 'ring of fellowship' that she and I were encircled by; indeed, this 'ring' was comprised of some very interesting and idiosyncratic fellow seekers (What Up to Jack, Sophia, Nils, Ariana, and Annmarie!). Ko Ko is also the one, perhaps not shockingly given her father's vocation, who sold me on the merits of astrology. I mean, I knew what astrology was. You couldn't make it through 1970s black America without repeatedly running into the question: "What's your sign?" But I doubted astrology's predictive efficacy, until she insisted that I give it a whirl, just like the ol' lady had done with *Vipassanā*. I muttered ornery, incredulous things about it before agreeing to give her my exact time, date, and place of birth. But she returned to me with my Zodiac chart; and really, I tell you, it was like looking into a mirror made of text. It was so dead-on that it made me mad—was she 'X-filing' me somehow? It took years of self-observation to confirm how accurate that chart really was, particularly the bits about money and the public's response to me; and it only gets more precise as the days unfold.

After a prolonged, wasting illness, that I faithfully tended to with grocery shopping, hospital trips, housecleaning, cat-feeding, plant-watering, and heaping helpings of hope, fear, and annoyance, she died in 2012. What snatched her away from us all too soon was a strange and rare bloodborne disease that only like three other people had ever contracted. *Sigh* Typical! It was only then that I realized she was pretty enamored with the darker side of things—occult domains I knew were powerful but appeared to me too malevolent to be toying with. In an unbearably delicate moment of holding her frail hand, while she was lying in her hospital bed, it occurred to me that I was looking at my best friend.

That same year, my aunty Kai, who'd seeded my mind with images of dynastic blackness, also transitioned to the ancestral realm. Sickness, death, and suffering! For crying out loud (bawling, actually), was that crazy monk ever wrong?

Thus it was when the dreadful date of December 21st, 2012 finally rolled around. At the risk of projecting my present awareness backward onto that windy winter day, I think I must have had an inarticulate general sense that, "If it's the end of the world, let's go ahead and get the fuck on with it." I distinctly remember feeling like I'd already lived through two of these 'end of civilization dates'—a fake, dry-run with 'Y2K,' and a very real 9/11; and by now if I wasn't necessarily good at it, I was definitely getting used to it at least. Accordingly, I decided to be somewhere close to home, where I could surf 'the net' if needed (if it was still available), but which was open and wide enough to afford an unobstructed view of the sky, in case the Mothership materialized. The obvious choice was Lake Merritt, which was right across the street from my flat. Meandering the lake's paths, while steeling myself against the drizzly spray and periodically craning my neck toward the clouds, for what seemed like hours, I psychically revisited the chaos, violence, sorrow, death, and ecological devastation I'd witnessed the last few years. Maybe this is really 'it'! Afterall, the world could be anything, including 'scheduled for demolition today.' I took note of moments of exaggeratedly odd mental and physical sensations. Am I getting vertigo? Everything looked yellow. I stumbled over a crack in the pavement, and a sharp pain shot up my back. Was I bugging? What if I was just hella turnt up for apocalyptic excitement? Or maybe the planets were lining up to do something outrageous? Would a black hole or stargate open and swallow the whole scene? What if we were already on the event horizon of a black hole and simply couldn't see it? After some indefinite period of this foolishness, dawn broke over Marblehead; and with no signs and wonders whatsoever forthcoming, I finally made my way back to my apartment, feeling mostly relieved, but ever-so-slightly disgusted. I turned on the TV—nothing, just the standard boilerplate. UGH!

Here's what's crazy though! I spent the rest of the next day puzzling frantically: 'What if, while I was wildin out, gawking at the sky, and putting too much on it, 'the job,' as it were, was done; and the new invisible paradigmatic hologram was slipped quietly into place, where and while nobody was looking. Not that I was anywhere near that lucid, all I could say, all I knew, was that I felt *different*.

2015

Now let's put some more in perspective
If total liberation be our objective
A variety of tools are effective
Some are outer focused, and some are reflective
India and China's Great Sage never wrote a page of text
But two and a half millennia later you can feel his effects
Every race, age, and sex,
Whether you idolize Marie Curie or Malcolm X
I'm talking about Siddhartha Gautama the Buddha
If you had a computer, you'd have been well advised to,
Recognize RZA breaking down the Heart Sutra
Shariputra got sonned to subsidize us in the future
No sight, no sound, no smell, no taste, no touch
No fight, no pound, no Hell, no chase, no clutch
No Dutchmaster, high priest or pastor
Neither slower or faster, before or after
Because the world's illusion
But just really persistent—Einstein, sorry for the confusion
Wait—let me back up: shit is real, but it seems
Completely convincing to journey
Through the realm of dreams
And all the time you just lying there, fast asleep
But inside your mind you're scaling buildings with one leap
Regaling millions, midnight creep and date mad cheap

Relative truth be superficial, absolute be mad deep
So do we know for sure, are we so secure
That this life is this life and nothing more?
Well I retain my right to disagree
And by the way, so do quantum physics and philosophy
And possibly, Gautama's biography
Encompasses the aforementioned, plus add on psychology
Maybe methodology, mystical astronomy, perhaps prophecy
Certainly ontology, pathology, biology
So what did he say? Ha ha! Okay
Blah-blah? No way, it's disarray
We mired in, ego fired in, cause we suffer
Can't do, don't like, never get enough of
The right kind, misaligned, turbulent mind
Our desires, halfhearted plus poorly defined
We're either: craving something, or pushing it away
What we don't want we get
What we want comes but won't stay
I wrote that like a decade ago
The question is: can I put in work and stay in the flow
But let go
Of the desire for quid-pro-quo?
As a youth the truth eluded me, but that kid did grow though
Subjected myself to hours of deep meditation
The veil was lifted, revealing interrelation
We still gotta move the nation
But for the sake of peace of mind,
Every now and then I dial up a different station
Channel Dharma, handle karma
The ego protects self about as stoutly as flannel armor

In other words, flimsy
These days my attitude is two parts urgent
Plus one part whimsy
But hey, don't take it from me
In closing I refer you to the master Bruce Lee
Who remarked: "Be like water my friend"
Does a million different things plus it knows how to blend
Meditation and martial arts be more than a trend
They both help you comprehend, they both help you ascend
The Middle Way is the path I'd recommend
Didn't mean to condescend, didn't mean to offend
~ the end ~

Writing this on New Year's Eve 2017, in placid, snow-blanketed Boulder, with *In a Sentimental Mood* on the radio, I'm appreciating the way an old email account can double as a virtual one-way time machine, and I can't help but reflect that I've endured some gnarly yearly transitions. Jeez! The three-year gap between the last chapter and this one has to do with the fact that in 2013 I was largely struggling to survive; and that struggle led very circuitously to Green Gulch, a branch of San Francisco Zen Center, and the de facto start of my surprisingly restless sojourn in the American Buddhist sangha. As it turned out, the 'dawning of the Age of Aquarius,' supposedly ushered in on December 21st 2012, but scarcely evident at the time, had some paradigm-shattering curve balls to lob at me after all.

Picking up where the story left off, I was doing hella much in 2013, and trying to get fellow students, faculty, and others on-board with my various unrealistic initiatives. An EBMC member told me about a website called Buddhist

Peace Fellowship. I tried to get a staff writing gig there, which didn't work out, but I did write a couple articles for them— "*Buddha Between Beats: Hip Hop Through a Dharma Lens,*" and "*By The Light of Buddha, I Navigate My Darkness.*" In the latter article, another person, a DJ, posted in the comments section that *he'd* been a fan and promoter of the Subterraneanz 'back in the day.' Yup! I was 'that dude.' I teamed with two black female students to form an 'African American Cultural Club' on campus; and we promoted it with an acapella performance of my KPFA song, at an event hosted by top Hip Hop journalist Davey D in the vestibule of Berkeley City College. Despite a very enthusiastic initial reception during 'Recruitment Week,' where we'd signed up more than fifty students, no more than five ever showed up to any meetings.

And on top of my obvious ineffectiveness at spearheading anything, my alleged and poorly defined 'power' was increasingly leaving me overcome by paranoia. What kind of 'power' was this? Who knew about it? Why? College campus-fueled paranoia in times of immense societal dislocation was not a new concept; I'd seen it over and over in the biographies of late 1960s Black Power activists and countercultural radicals. But these people were involved in active, visible movements; and shit, I could barely sustain an email dialogue with one person, never mind mobilize enough people for a movement. Nonetheless, in the wake of the Occupy Movement, I had a feeling I was continuously getting caught up in weird, 'deep-state,' protest-suppression tactics being clandestinely tested across the city. One day, a guy walked past me twice, mean-mugging me like he was spoiling for a fight. Another time, I was the only passenger on a city bus, and the driver refused to let me off at my stop. Agents in cars and on bicycles snapped my picture as they rode by; or did they? I was noticing what seemed to be rolling containment zones, conducted by scowling men, around Lake Merritt; or was I? Were these incidents coincidental or connected? Was it simply that "my mind is playing tricks on me," as the Geto Boys entertainingly put it? Was the crashing and bashing coming from adjacent and overhead apartments just random disturbance, or something more nefarious? What was going on with traffic cameras and electronic devices at the intersections? Why is this lady looking in my window from the driveway of the house next door? Everything felt hostile and covert, with invisible eyes and scheming brains all around. On one spectacularly frazzled full-moon night, I shaved my head to 'change my appearance;' and looking in the mirror, seeing buzzed-off afro puffs clinging to my ears, I said to my disheveled reflection, half-solemnly and half hysterically: *"Okay bruh. You're going mad again. Remember how this works?"*

In the Spring semester of '13, I took a Buddhist Philosophy class, where I heard for the first time that people lived and worked in American Buddhist sanghas. With a snowballing sense of urgency, I began frantically contacting sanghas (Dharma College, Nyingma Institute, Ratna Ling, Chagdud Gompa, Medicine Buddha, Tzu Chi, et al.); because after over a decade of tolerant generosity, my landlady had finally tired of my delinquency and was starting eviction proceedings. Shit was getting *real!* I'd spent nearly twenty years in this flat, after first living there with two other members of the Exile Society, shortly after we arrived in Oakland in 1995; and now I needed a new place to live, and was utterly insolvent.

'The Center for Economic Policy and Research' issued a report that year showing that black college graduates were twice as likely to be unemployed, due to employers refusing to call-back candidates whose names sounded 'ethnic' . . . like 'Kyva.' The factoid that really stuck with me was that 'white men with recent criminal histories are far more likely to receive calls back than black men with no criminal record at all.' And there I was with barely enough credits for an associate's degree. W.T.F! By any measure, my life had somehow become unmanageable. I wanted to run from it screaming, but not without a roof to run back under! So when I set out 'seeking refuge in the Buddha, Dharma, and Sangha,' it wasn't at all metaphoric—it was literal.

The first sangha to have me was a Tendai Buddhist Monastery, with two monks, in Middleton, a short distance from Harbin Hot Springs resort. Although I'd hit it off nicely with the abbot, he spazzed out on me after a freaky night where I'd slipped into meditative absorption: a state as close to true *vipassanā* as I'd had since my initial retreat. I then found the 'Padmasambhava Peace Institute' in Santa Rosa, which was housed in a former prison-reform complex, and gave them a whirl. Again: after positive initial contact with the recruiter, I met the facility directors, and things went south. One of the directors, after hearing that I was from Boston, remarked that he remembered the *forced bussing crisis'* of 1974 . . . the very same vicious assault incident that I'd lived through, known as *'school desegregation'* by the residents of Roxbury, Dorchester, and Mattapan, who sought non-dilapidated education for their children. From that point onward, I had reason to suspect race would be a factor in my acceptance or rejection by the community; and that's exactly how it happened. This person and another white male, after a strenuous attempt on my part to be helpful and effective on the grounds, concluded that I was being 'unprofessional.' Unprofessional butter lamp cleaning, making beds, and weeding? THAT– would be coded language. No explanation was ever offered as to what I was doing wrong. I emailed the recruiter asking her what happened, and she acted like she had no idea what I was talking about.

Green Gulch Farms is a traditional Japanese style monastery, tucked away in an almost absurdly photogenic unincorporated section of Marin County, about 20 minutes by car outside of San Francisco through iconically twisty Northern California mountain roads. To arrive there is, in some noticeable sense, to have left the 'real world' behind, especially with the fog rolling in. Exquisitely tended grounds, verdant and productive fields and gardens, cradled by lazy hills unfolding out to a small beach, the ambient environment was perfectly suited to quiet, serious contemplation. The grounds included a fully-equipped teahouse, woodworking and mechanical facilities, conference rooms, a library, bookstore, dining hall, and bakery, all in meticulously unadorned, wooden Japanese architecture, replete with *bonsho* and *densho* bells. Altogether, it imparted a subtle but profound message about uncluttered, reverent self-reliance and the inherent basic goodness of humans working humbly with nature to create mindful harmony. Less than a month before I was to be evicted, I stepped out of my cab, on the first night of a twelve-day trial stay on a general work crew, and said to myself: '*finally*, I've happened upon a reasonable way to live.' Well, 'third time's the charm,' as the saying goes. The thoughtful residents of Green Gulch were as sweetly hospitable and accommodating as the land itself. I couldn't have scripted a more pleasant and invigorating stay (although I'd indeed imagined what it might be like to find a remnant of countercultural late-1960s communal living somewhere in the Bay Area). It felt apropos.

When the community decided it would have me, I returned to Oakland and my quickly dissolving former life with a sense that there was a narrow way forward. But I still had to work out the details of my closing chapter in the spirited, radical, majority-black city I'd come to love so fiercely. Curiously, this somehow included playing keyboards in a funk band that I'd been corralled into by Subterraneanz fan and talented local guitarist, Brother Reggie. It had been years since I performed professionally, and I was simultaneously packing my meager belongings to vacate the premises before the County got involved. If the band could have fronted me several thousand dollars—not that I was anywhere near that competent on my instrument—I might've stayed on with them. It would have been a pretty dope outfit to play with, 'town business' all-day long! Instead, I ended up recruiting Brother Reggie to be my sole assistant in loading my stuff onto a moving truck. In between trips of heaving precariously unraveling cardboard boxes back and forth in the pouring rain, I'd periodically look out on what was left of the backyard, where the Subterraneanz had held musical court so many years ago; seeing the trees cut down, grapevines torn out, and the concrete dug up and strewn about, I thought how melancholic and poetic it all was.

I went directly from my storage unit to the Greyhound bus terminal, for a short stay at my mother's place in Pasadena, home of the jet propulsion laboratory in Los

Angeles County; and from there, I came right back to the Bay to get on with my new life as a monk. I'm not being cheeky here; anyone who's spent time at a monastery knows it to be a full-time, full-on affair, not for the faint of heart. The mandatory daily schedule starts with a *tenken*, where a resident monk literally runs through the grounds ringing a loud bell at 4:20 in the morning. Rolling out of bed, you immediately proceed to the *zendo*, a large traditional meditation hall, for your morning sit, or *zazen*. Adopting a dignified, upright posture on your *zafu*, your circular meditation cushion, you lower your gaze, take some deep, vitalizing breaths, and start meditating. After sitting, *sutras*, Buddhist scriptures, and other chants are recited in English and Japanese. Then, residents perform temple service (cleaning the *zendo*, bathrooms, showers, entrances, walkways, etc.) and have breakfast, followed by a brief rest period. At 8:30, there's a mandatory work circle, where important community announcements are made, and then the actual workday begins. Some are on gardening crews or general labor crews; others are farming, grounds keeping, and doing different tasks. I started out on a general labor crew and was later moved to the kitchen. My job as a cook was extensive. We not only handled preparing gourmet vegetarian meals for an exacting public, while observing strict safety and hygiene codes; we also participated in regular kitchen-shrine services and offerings (with chants and readings of the Zen classic the *Tenzokyokun*, or *Instructions to the Cook*), and attended exhaustive staff meetings about performance, morale, and how it all relates to the teachings of various Japanese and Chinese ancestors. Aside from the morning routine and workday, the monastic schedule included more meditation and chanting before lunch, dinner, and bedtime at 8:00 pm, attending regular dharma talks and nightly classes, and two hours of community farming every Wednesday. Additionally, everyone is required to learn and practice the serving and eating arts of *oriyoki*, ritual collective dining, using personalized nested bowls and chopsticks; and there are seven-day *sesshins*, intensive meditation retreats, as well as numerous ceremonial observances, which all residents are required to perform. All of it, mind you, is highly structured, ritualized, and formal in accord with the Zen Buddhist tradition. Most of what you do is tightly controlled, and fairly closely scrutinized. You're walking a privileged path in an esteemed ascetic lineage, once only open to a tiny minority. You are thus charged with putting your good karma in the service of liberating all sentient beings, at all times.

Coming face-to-face with yourself during practice, which you discover, in short order, happens unceasingly, will most assuredly become maddening at some point. Oh, fickle, trembling weapon: mind! Meditation is only medicine. The whole point of sangha is that you're contained and supported in your inevitable unraveling by a community of attentive *bodhisattvas* (at one or another level of attainment), who can gingerly help steer you back to the Middle Way with wisdom, compassion, and skillful means. That's the idea, anyways.

A few weeks into my residency, the implanted lens in my right eye failed, just as the last doctor to operate on my eyes warned me it would; and since I already couldn't see out of my left eye, I was completely blind. Caught between feeling cursed, tortured, doomed, and grateful that at least it happened in a responsive community, I struggled, with dedicated assistance from a few residents, to apply for health insurance and have an operation; and I got one. A few days later, my sight was not improving, and I went back for a checkup, only to find out I'd gotten an eye infection and needed immediate medical attention. The ophthalmologist said it was a good thing I didn't wait or second guess, or else I would have lost the eye entirely. An antibiotic injection resolved the problem, but at the monastery, I was confined to bed for twenty hours a day, as I was required to keep my head parallel with the floor for two weeks. During that time, a seven-day *sesshin* was in session, making the grounds utterly silent throughout most of it; and being immobile in bed and unable to look around, I drifted routinely into delirious terror. I couldn't account for where I was; was this a Bay Area monastery in the 21st century? a ravaged, abandoned WWII field hospital (which seemed especially possible when someone with a German accent would finally speak)? or some kind of *bardo*, a purgatory in an alternate dimension? As I started to recover after two weeks of bed confinement, I slowly and tentatively rose and walked around the room, finally venturing outside during a downpour. Clutching an umbrella in one hand, and groping about in the dark for handrails with the other, I pushed forward onto the once familiar steep paths around the dormitory, which were now a slippery, dangerous, black blur. Gradually, a powerful real-time meditation began to emerge: different senses kicked in; sounds from the creek running nearby gave me previously unnoticed information on where I was; and a few bulbs along the bottom of a sheltered *zendo* walkway made me mindful of, and thankful for, the little light that was shining.

After regaining full sight in my right eye, life more or less settled into the regimented predictability of the schedule. Zen is not playtime! It's earnest, serious business, and 'Zennies' have a well-deserved reputation for understated, gracious composure, and attention to detail. At the same time, it also has a reputation for being, as Western Buddhist popularizer and 'spiritual entertainer' Alan Watts put it, a 'hoax;' with a canon filled of anecdotes about revered ancestor monks clowning, smacking up, and throwing things at each other, and referring to the Tathagata, the Blessed One himself, as 'dried dung' and 'shit stick.' What the hell is going on here? Truthfully, I'm reluctant to say! As Watts and others have attested, nobody really knows what Zen is; nobody really knows what quantum physics is, either . . . hmm. As so many times before in this book, I could burn through pages and pages trying to come up with an elaborate, *sutra*-like exposition on the subject. Instead, mostly as an exercise in compact preciseness, I'll use more of a koan-like approach.

What Zen appears to be is a certain supple elasticity of thought, which is only possible when the mind is completely relaxed. But this relaxation isn't lazy or tuned out in the least. It's precisely the result of rigorous training and strong determination to apprehend every imaginable angle and subtlety of any given thing, and then *let go;* because in fact, *the world could be anything.* Who knows what's gonna come at you? Why be anywhere but present, accounted for, psychically loose, and limber enough to respond? What separates an ordinary musician from, say, a John Coltrane-level master, is that the master player has learned and drilled in the craft of jazz, so thoroughly they are prepared to relax in any performance environment; the pitch, scale, tempo, timbre, volume, chords, intervals, scales, key signatures, phrasing, rhythm, melody, and harmony of jazz are all integrated inside of them. They never sound anything but brilliant—whether they're toodling around for themselves in an underground walkway, playing for a few friends in a living room, rehearsing with a very tight quartet in a sound studio, or onstage with a carefree 'space-rock jamband' with a slightly out of tune bassist. It doesn't matter whether their horn is top of the line or fresh from the pawn shop, whether they're congested or cold, they're just . . . READY. So, a Zen teacher tries to trick you, or hustle you, out of your rigidly dualistic habitual mind, by responding to questions, for which you already have a fixed expectation, with answers that defy logic and seemingly have nothing to do with the question. This is not out of malice, but because the master knows that you're asking the question from a place of deep, inarticulate discomfort, born of mental constipation which can't be softened with more tension and discomfort-producing thought like the answer you're expecting. You must drop all assumptions about how the world works to directly experience how it actually works, *as it is;* and to be sufficiently rehearsed in conditions 'just as they are,' you must pay close attention to the transient, shifting, illusory nature of phenomena. Just when you think you've 'got it' . . . oops, slipping away! The stillness of a pacified mind is likened to the reflective surface of a pond, which is perfectly itself, and yet, completely free to hold the image of any creature flying over it. The Buddha famously never entertained inquiries into the nature of God, or the origins of the universe, because merely having the question is to suffer from a mind already churning like the surface of a pond blown by hurricane winds. *You are asking about*

God from a desire for relief and comfort that's born of clinging and craving; and you'd be better served confronting this desire directly. Zen is, therefore, filled with exercises, stories, contemplations, poems, techniques, and ruses to reconfigure the mind, so that it produces as few distracting artifacts as possible. Stripped of preconceived notions, things might present themselves to perception and be received as they exist inherently, not as they 'might be' or 'should be.' And since one thus self-realized knows they're not separate from anyone else, that all existence interpenetrates, the compassion, wisdom and skillful means brought to bear on one's own circumstances is effortlessly brought to bear on the not-separate circumstances of others; hence, the bodhisattva.

To contextualize this, here's a brief excursion into Buddhist history.

100 or so years after Siddhartha's death, or *parinirvana,* sometime in the 4th century B.C.E (Before the Common Era, according to the Julian/Babylonian calendar), his teachings at last began to be copied down in foundational Sanskrit and Pali texts like the *Abhidharma* (About Dharma) — a fascinating, infuriatingly complex, and arcane textbook of basic Buddhist abstractions I'd love to rant and rave over, were it not far beyond the necessary scope of this book. As with all originating spiritual revelation however, disagreements over meaning and local cultural adaptations began to spin Dharma into various, sometimes incompatible, forms.

For convoluted reasons I won't get into and probably don't understand anyway, the early Sri Lankan Theravada tradition, whose practical basis was the bareboned technique of 'insight meditation' or *vipassanā*, spread throughout Southeast Asia, in Thailand, Cambodia, Laos, Myanmar, Singapore, and Malaysia, between 200 B.C.E and 200 C.E. This tradition held that the highest level of attainment was that of an *arhat*, a solitary sagely master, also known by his beloved Western cliché, 'the bearded man in a cave.' Having handily dispatched suffering and all its attendant causes and conditions—defeating the Great Wheel of Samsara, the bane of all ages of all sorts and types, stretching back to the earliest, most primordial of proto-eons — the arhat, pleased with himself, is all like: "*Okay you know what? I'm GOOD! For real, for real. Um . . . e-yeah. Good luck with that . . .*" and taps out. Not everyone agreed with that Dharma, that Way. Northern Buddhism–and some may have read intriguing books, like *The Gods of Northern Buddhism*, featuring mysteriously provocative place names like 'Samb(h)o' — articulated the position of Mahayana, the Great Vehicle, which had as its ideal a much more world concerned, people-oriented level of attainment: the *bodhisattva*. In response to the arhat's stance, the *bodhisattva's* all like: "*Damn yo! You HELLA selfish. Bruh, see all these people out here trippin all over the place? You don't care about none of that?*" This variant went to East Asia, spreading through China, Korea,

Japan, and Mongolia. Very consequently, it also went to Tibet, but that's getting ahead in the story.

Remember now: everywhere these traditions go, they diversify (or maybe 'mutate') due to local cultures, interpretations, and disagreements. I should mention here that the generally agreed-upon timeline is that archaic Buddhism was in existence in Sri Lanka sometime in the 4th century B.C.E., and then traveled North and mutated before reaching China for the first time around 68 C.E. Sometime in the early 5th century C.E., a variant of the Mahayana tradition called 'Ch'an' (or 'Zen') emerged in China, whose initial proponent was a *very* surly individual, named Bodhidharma — an Indian monk with a giant bird's-nest-beard, crazed eyes, a lot to say, and apparently, some badass martial arts skills on the down-low. China's primal Buddhism and Bodhidharma's Ch'an, between 420 and 537 C.E., spawned various local adaptations: Shingon, Soen, Tanghi, Th'ien, and Nichiren — which started out as Tiantai, or 'Tendai,' as in the first Zen, or Zen-like monastery I went into, which in fact practiced a vigorous and strenuous form of arhat monasticism (Gassho, VK). Anyway, more adaptations and Northeast migration happened, and during the Kamakura Era of Japan, 1192-1333 C.E., the teachings of Bodhidharma and Ch'an fell into the hands of a monk named Dogen, who is considered the ultimate patriarch of Japanese Zen.

Now! There's plenty to say about *that*. But to keep it popping, let's just go ahead and zip forward a little to the late 19th and early 20th century. As a response to disaster and carnage wrought by European industrialism and imperialism, certain European mystic-intellectuals began to imagine ways to draw these teachings, along with others now considered sufficiently ancient, into the modern world, whose post-modern period we are living through now. This collective genre of wisdom was known by the name Theosophy, and was associated with mystics such as Alice Bailey, Annie Besant, Madame Blavatsky, Rudolf Steiner, et al. Coincidentally, Theosophy's list of proponents includes the name of one Paschal Beverly Randolph, a *sorely* underrecognized magician, high priest-like master practitioner of Tantra, and mulatto black man who, you know, just happens to be a progenitor of the movement Theosophy would mutate into a.k.a. the New Age. As part of the New Age movement, you had younger, hipper (in some cases much too hip) philosopher-mystic-intellects, like those I've been prattling on about in this text, (Manly P Hall, for example, a 33rd degree Mason who taught all the way from the early-to-late 20th century). Pierre Teilhard de Chardin could certainly be cited as a significant part of this pantheon also (see the chapter on 2012). At some point between the early 1900s and 1950s, archaic Theosophy/New Age thought, very much fused with, and infused by, Zen and other forms of Buddhism, was subjected to copious amounts of hallucinogens and other narcotics, causing it to transmogrify (sorry about this glob of a word) into the the late 1960s counterculture movement, starring such luminaries as Alan Watts, Timothy Leary, Terence McKenna, and many others I haven't mentioned.

Alan Watts, the charismatic alcoholic wordsmith with the tonally posh London accent and hyper-clear insight, is in fact interred on the grounds of Green Gulch. In addition to a few sublimely solemn ceremonial visits to the gravesite of San Francisco Zen Center founder, and author of the seminal text *Zen Mind Beginner's Mind,* a farseeing bodhisattva in his own right, the Honorable Shunryu Suzuki-ji (big *gasshos* to him), the Senior Dharma instructor of the monastery, Tenzin Roshi, led one rather raucous procession of us worker-bees to Watts's burial place, about a mile and a half up and down a brambly, semi-treacherous hill path. We need to move on, although I could drone on endlessly about the mind warping psycho-spiritual encounters I had during my nearly year-and-a-half residency at Green Gulch: animal-to-human telepathy, epiphany mixing on the beach with Buddhists and non-Buddhists alike in the 'real' world of wealthy Marin County, epic, in some cases nearly deadly, mountain hikes (including one where the faces of familial ancestors literally blew in off the ocean out of the fog), moments of guitar-canoodling brilliance, spooky, spacey moments on moonlit paths, sunstroke, meditative flights of ecstasy, despair, horror, and cooking altered-state-inducing meals on the orders of voices in my head, etc.

But let's keep it kicking. To zoom the lens out for a minute: what's happening here is that, after an *arhat*-style awakening in Theravadin *vipassanā*, a *Hinayana* ('small vehicle'—a prickly point of inter-Buddhist tension) tradition, I had entered a *bodhisattva* practice in Zen, a *Mahayana* ('great vehicle') tradition. And by that time, an interesting and dynamic picture was developing, displaying why things were unfolding as they were. Postmodern American Buddhism, largely a product of late-1960s/early-1970s counterculture, has been an overwhelmingly white, middle-class phenomenon. And although Buddha Dharma is increasingly a draw for African Americans (to return to a theme from the introduction of this book), a racialized, when not overtly racist, streak of colonialism endures in Buddhism, as it does of course, in society-at-large.

Now, I know this is not going to be the most comforting subject to go into; but if Siddhartha, Bodhidharma, and Dogen's Mahayanist mission and vision of enlightened liberation for all beings is to have any hope of being realized, the American Buddhist sangha will need to develop the courage to address racism, classism, sexism, genderism, etc. with much more systematized vigor than it's currently summoning. Did I say that emphatically enough? This was my primary takeaway from San Francisco Zen Center; although I will immediately qualify that by saying I am not, in any shape or form, condemning anybody I met in Zen as a racist, even though I have met what I'd call 'suspected' or 'potential racists' in Buddhist sanghas. The residents of Green Gulch, and the members of the larger umbrella organization, San Francisco Zen Center, generally speaking, are, well, my friends, my honest colleagues and allies for whom I have great regard. They offered me refuge—

comparatively luxurious refuge at that—at a moment in my life where I would have otherwise been functionally homeless. But my abiding respect is also informed by my own direct experience, as well as experiences that I've observed of other African American disciples of Siddhartha. If I were to sum up, in a single word, what I find the issue to be, that word would be: *marginalization*.

I will not, at this point, go into details of the racial profiling incident at the beach in Green Gulch, or the spiritually-bypassed neglect that caused a black woman to hurl a half-full pot of oatmeal at the wall in protest (which *I* found pretty hip). Nor will I catalog the many microaggressions I incurred personally at Green Gulch, as I did in a letter to the community upon departing. A single illustrative anecdote will suffice.

The Northern California winter in 2014 was exceedingly warm and dry: after raining heavily as expected during December, January came and went without so much as a drop of precipitation; in February, it rained for a week; in March, nothing; in April, there was exactly one weekend of rain. And during that time, I was feeling besieged and fatigued by reports of extrajudicial police killings of black Americans, psy-op rap music, transhumanism, and resurgent, national, racial strife (which Zen was not up to responding to coherently, beyond grieving). And my mind was also racing with unconventional new insights, which I was expounding in the form of essays (with titles like 'What's a Black Bodhisattva to Do,' 'Thought Forms,' 'Shamanic Black Buddhism,' 'Four Quantum Noble Truths,' and 'Quantum Effects are Visible in the Observable World'). This last one, I emailed to Dr. Dean Radin, senior scientist at the Institute of Noetic Studies (IONS), who gave a brief but illuminating response. Anyway, by the time I found myself in a seven-day winter sesshin, I was so distraught over the seemingly irredeemable degeneracy of the world that I'd actually considered ritual immolation; I even started a strange self-justifying manuscript called 'Son of Revolutionary Suicide,' the sentiments of which are in this book. My sit, perhaps unsurprisingly, was thus tormented by spontaneous fits of 'Post Traumatic Slave Syndrome.' What arose, staring at the wall, was a near-suffocating sense of utter powerlessness, amplified by the sight of a heavy metal chain underneath a tree during my practice of 'fast *kinhin*,' or meditative circumambulation of the *zendo*. After walking past it several times, and having it plague me with images of black bodies in chains, I stepped out from the line of shuffling meditators, knelt down beside the tree, and settled the chain on my forearm; the weight and pinch of my skin gave me a tactile experience of what I was going through mentally. It was a moment of deep ancestral connection through pain. But very quickly, the *tanto* (the 'head of the Tan' or 'chief officer in charge of monk training') ran up to me in a bug-eyed, agitated, panicky huff, like: "Um... Kyva could you *please* get back in line?!" Seconds later, a nice white woman drifted out of the shuffling line to look out over the courtyard, and this same *tanto* approached her and asked her to rejoin the line; but in contrast with the frustration he showed when requesting the same of me, this time, he was very cordial, and smiled relaxedly, with hands folded in a bow.

That year, I attended a meeting of black Buddhists in San Francisco and heard tale after tale of microaggressions and unacknowledged white privilege, fragility, and spiritual bypass. In a nutshell, the problem is this: Buddhism's interesting capacity to adapt to and accommodate local causes and conditions has not been fully realized in America—not even close. Unless American sanghas take more than a cosmetic stance on diversity and social justice, like the East Bay Meditation Center does, they will be, on the whole, places where, if articles in the monthly glossies are correct, even Asians from Buddhist countries will feel uncomfortable and unwelcome (rendering the sangha another sorry site of entrenched colonialism).

Getting back to work on this book, after treating myself to a nice sushi dinner celebrating my 49th year on the planet as a 'skin-encapsulated ego,' I see, in hindsight, that incompatible cultural dynamics of collectivism and individualism were also at play there. Historical Zen is situated in a collectivist Japanese culture, whereas American sanghas are situated within an individualist cultural orbit, rooted in Western European thinking. A convincing argument could be made that African Americans, while definitely influenced by America's individualist culture, have a largely collectivist cultural orientation. This can be witnessed in many memes: in popular sayings like 'all we got is us,' in the feeling that we're always 'representing the race' whether we like it or not, in the way we talk about O.J, Oscar Grant, Oprah, and Omarosa like distant relatives, in the way the black conscious community addresses its online audience as 'family,' etc. White Buddhists can envision a collectivist, diverse, and equitable American sangha that's more faithful to Buddhism's original, collectivist, Asian cultural contexts; but because of America's well established racial history, they are less able to deal with individual black Americans coming out of their own particular collectivist culture. Therefore, white allies can accept responsibility for diversity and equity in public collective spaces, but find it more difficult in private and intensely personal settings with individual black people; and furthermore, the potential emotional volatility, due to the collectivized suffering of black people involved in these discussions, only makes fruitful engagement that much more unlikely. Thus, unless a determined, rigorous, and honest racial dialogue is sustained within a sangha, white leadership can shut down and/or tune-out (spiritually bypass) engagement, allowing everyone to retreat into psychic environments where stereotypes and illusory demons are never exposed to scrutiny. In the white mind, an individual black person is thus reflexively subsumed into an abstracted collective 'blackness'; and likewise, in the black mind, an individual white person is reflexively subsumed into an abstracted, collective 'whiteness.' Both minds think *they're all alike,* which is, of course, false. This is an important point, so I hope I'm not screwing it up!

All that said, my critique of race relations in Zen was not enough to make me leave Green Gulch. It was at least a place where people were *trying,* where profound transformative practice was not only encouraged, but required and expected, and where you went to sleep and awoke in a veritable paradise, with three sumptuous healthy meals a day, amid ancient redwoods, fog-shrouded hills, and a beach down the road. Leaving, in fact, was a very grueling decision to make. The climate, of all things, is what finally tipped the scales. I was ironically feeling oppressed by the sun, and unendurably creeped out over the dwindling creek running through the land, conflicts between the kitchen, garden, and farm over water usage, seemingly drooping vegetation, and dusty soil. It was like seeing, in real time, the grim, desiccated future Jeremy Rifkin had predicted fifteen years prior in his book 'Entropy.' I was recognizing the extent to which I was still a New Englander, expecting, and even preferring, cold, snowy winters. So when I came across photos of a single, massive, color-splashed stupa with snow-covered mountain peaks in the background, I knew instantly that it ought to be my next destination.

After calling Green Gulch Farms 'home' from early 2014 to the summer of 2015, I boarded a plane to go live and work at the place whose photo so attracted me, Shambhala Mountain Center (SMC), in Colorado. Before traversing the cloudy ceiling, I stared down pensively upon a rather brown, dry-looking Bay Area, not a hundred percent convinced I'd ever return. When the plane dipped below the cloud line again, outside of Denver, I sighed heavily with relief at the sight of flat and abundantly green terrain stretching out in all directions.

Now, *Shambhala*, afterwhich the retreat center was named, was not an alien term to me; I'd heard of the ancient mythical kingdom, where a perfected humankind allegedly survives somewhere in a *terra incognita* of the Himalayan mountains. From time to time, I even dreamed absentmindedly of what it might be like to live there. I was also familiar, from my New Age investigation days, with the name of the iconoclastic monk who'd founded the retreat center, and brought the curious concept of 'crazy wisdom' to the West, Chogyam Trungpa Rinpoche. But nothing could have prepared me for the initial approach to Shambhala Mountain Center, 8000 feet up in the tiny town of Red Feather Lakes. Driving up the long, slight gradient into the Rocky Mountains and Roosevelt National Forest, you could fuck around and assume you were on your way to the real Shambhala. I'd never before seen light, bushes, water, rocks, and trees in that configuration, in that relationship, at least not in person. Distant 'dragon-spine mountaintops' glimmered and shimmered against the rolling blue, gray, and orange sunset sky, with rushing rapids hugging the foothills along the highway. So excellent! Ascending slowly, sitting back contentedly in my seat, I imagined I might already be getting a touch of the ol' crazy wisdom my-damn-self, like: "Huh . . . I'm getting good at this!"

As it turned out, 'basic goodness' was the name of the game at Shambhala Mountain Center (again, *in theory*). In his many books and talks, Trungpa described basic goodness as the fact that all of life—everywhere, at all times—is auspicious, favorably conditioned, or at the very least, 'workable.' The Earth is brimming with radiant possibilities for positive evolution, growth, and transcendence. Even negative, or indeed disastrous, circumstances contain within them the seeds of better, happier outcomes. So the idea is to become sensitive to evermore subtle gradations of 'basic goodness.' Is this fundamental truth, in one way or another, not in evidence always? For instance, my parents used to tell us kids that "a negative is only trying to become a positive." Pssh—they were shamans; in spite of not knowing it, or accepting any descriptor like that, their teachings are precisely the reason my life unfolded as it did. Anyway, a need to identify basic goodness was front and center right off the rip. When Green Gulch Senior Dharma teacher Tenzin Roshi described the land at SMC as "even more beautiful than here," in addition to not thinking of it as a contest in the first place, I didn't exactly believe it was possible; I did when I got there, however. But this setting was much more . . . 'rustic' than anything I'd ever called home before. To keep it a buck, when first arriving at the compound, I had a flashing twinge of, "Yikes, what have I gotten myself into?!" Living at Green Gulch, in bucolic unincorporated Marin had already shown me how much of a city cat I really was. But now, I was looking at residents living in mobile homes, and in what are damn near log cabins. Well, I exhaled another great sigh of relief when I arrived 'downtown,' where the nicer modern buildings were, and found out I'd be staying in one of the guest lodges. (Later, I was moved to the log cabin). Another chance to practice basic goodness dharma came, when I, after asking my supervisor about the rules of the job, was told: "Don't have sex with participants, and technically weed is forbidden on the land."

Okay, 'Don't have sex with participants and technically weed is forbidden on the land.' Here's the thing: I'd just spent nearly a year and a half in a kitchen with very strict and exact protocols for *everything*. I'd gotten used to checking, mostly myself, on adherence to the Buddha Way in all matters of work, and appreciated the discipline. And now I was being told that virtually anything goes? That was disconcerting; and it wasn't the only thing either. The Shambhala lineage has its own colorful, unique, and evocative take on Buddha Dharma, including many lovely ceremonies, rituals, and chants; although I found myself preferring the stripped-down, straightforward language of the Zen Heart Sutra to the wordier, more flowery Shambhala text. And attendance at all these ceremonies, rituals, text recitations, etc. are *completely voluntary*—either you practice them, or, you know, whatever. Instead of regular check-ins and interviews with senior staff to monitor progress, you were pretty much on your own to hold yourself to practice standards (or not); most communication was done through email, and there was exactly one community-meeting per week. Furthermore, *this* kitchen handled and served meat, and I mean fresh, high quality, vegetarianism-annihilating meat (although I still cringed imagining handling it). I'll go ahead and qualify these observations by adding that SMC was clearly not designed to be a monastic environment; it is a convention/retreat/camping center staffed by residents. Hidden in the arrangement, however, is a very deep, elusive, and powerful spiritual principle, whose concealment could certainly be thought of as part of the practice. Out of respect for the historical context from which these once highly-guarded esoteric teachings derive, I will only give a brief sketch of what I under, over, and inner-stand, as it relates to information readily available in the public domain.

As I mentioned earlier, a *Mahayana* version of Buddhism arrived in Tibet between the 7th and 9th centuries C.E. Tibet already had a much older indigenous, animistic, shamanic spiritual tradition called Bon, which has an elusive and possibly controversial provenance (that I'd love to go into were it not, again, far beyond the necessary scope of this book). If you're intrigued enough, I might suggest looking into the works of E. A. Wallis Budge, William Flinders Petrie, Godfrey Higgins (*Anacalypsis*), and Gerald Massey (*Ancient Egypt: Light of the World*), as well as mind-melting discoveries of Egyptian and Buddhist artifacts in the Grand Canyon and throughout the Americas, and correspondence between, for example, the "42 Negative Confessions of Ma'at" of the *Egyptian Book of the Dead*, and the "42 Peaceful Deities" of the *Tibetan Book of the Dead*, which apparently includes the 'Seven Buddhas before Buddha,' whom are paid homage in Zen. Be advised: such an investigation may force you to reevaluate everything you think you know about world history. Keeping it kicking though: Buddha Dharma and Bon were synthesized into what we now call Tibetan Buddhism, or *Vajrayana* (the 'diamond or thunderbolt vehicle,' also known as 'Esoteric Buddhism,' or 'Buddhist Tantra'). From what I can tell, there is a scholarly consensus that the three *yanas*, or vehicles—*Hinayana, Mahayana,* and *Vajrayana*—exist exactly in that order to express ideal stages of opening to progressively deeper, and therefore more potentially hazardous, occult practices, presumably involving, among other things, the development of *siddhis*, or supernatural powers. It makes a lot of sense, therefore, to enter a Buddhist practice at the *Hinayana* level, studying and working with basic causes and conditions, suffering, the Eightfold Path, foundational mind training, etc.; and from there, to continue along the path at a *Mahayana* level, where other sentient beings and their causes and conditions, suffering, and liberational longings might be met and responded to mindfully—in preparation for a *Vajrayana* level characterized by the practice of *Dzogchen* (the Great Perfection) or *Mahamudra* (the Great Seal), a state of primordial being where everyday life and formal practice are indistinguishable. By way of simile: the *Hinayana* is kind of like discovering you have a bicycle, a road, and a destination; the *Mahayana* is like taking off down the road on a bicycle with training wheels, amongst other cyclists of varying skill; and finally, the *Vajrayana* is like having the bicycle under your arse metamorphose into a jet-powered miniature plane. You get why you need caution and preparation? The clearer you see things, the more you realize the world could be anything; the more emotional, mental, physical, and spiritual command you acquire, the greater the reach of your psychic-energetic (or morphogenic) field of influence. And as the saying goes: with great power comes great responsibility.

And speaking of 'power,' various experiences at SMC started to clarify and contextualize the strange affect I noted in the previous chapter, the way people perceived me as 'scary,' 'overwhelming,' etc. It was fitting that the setting was not a monastery, but something closer to the 'real world,' a place of everyday encounter, employment, and engagement, which just happened to be Buddhist-themed, as it was not properly Buddhist, since practice was not enforced while I was there.

Esoteric Buddhism, or Vajrayana Tantra, is an exceedingly rarefied platform to operate upon that doesn't necessarily scream out its presence in a crowded room; thus many people delude themselves into thinking they're 'really doing it.' In the dining hall, I would hear whispers about this or that person supposedly carrying on with advanced shenanigans on the down-low. *sigh* Were they? Really? Now, far be it for me to question anyone's practice, like "oh yeah, look at me, I'm this ascended tantric master." That's not what I'm saying; I'm not sure how I'd even conclusively know if I was a 'master.' The world could be anything. At the same time, it dawned on me that, without exactly intending to or consciously willing it, I'd indeed progressed through the three sequential stages: awakening at *Vipassanā* (*Hinayana*), living as a monk at Green Gulch (*Mahayana*), and winding up in the mythical kingdom of Shambhala (*Vajrayana*). Do you see what's going on here, in terms of the overall theme of hybridity, evolution, and the Buddha Dharma?

On the wall of the kitchen office, there was a placard with a picture of the rascally old monk, Trungpa, and the following provocation offered below:

> *Born a monk,*
> *Died a king,*
> *Such a thunderstorm does not stop;*
> *We will be haunting you*
> *Along with the dralas,*
> *Jolly good luck*

'Huh? What?!' is what I thought when first seeing it. 'The nerve of this guy! Pssh. That's how you feel?' By the end of my nearly one and a half years at SMC (exactly the amount of time, interestingly enough, I'd called Green Gulch 'home'), I knew exactly what he meant. And this, at long last, brings me to the song starting this chapter. It was an update of the verse from 'the Black Bodhisattva' I started the 2006 chapter with; in it, I attempted to integrate and summarize, in the best way I knew how, what I was working with in 2015—power, *zazen*, nonattachment, ambient awareness, basic goodness, crazy-wisdom, tightly-worded poetry, self-discipline, extraordinary joy at small things, dream yoga, humor, philosophy, etc.

I've worked quite hard to not make this a scurrilous tell-all scandal sheet 'exposing' American Buddhism. And keeping with that effort, I won't provide an itemized list of the microaggressions, privilege, and fragility I incurred at Shambhala Mountain Center. But they were there in abundance, as well as examples of flat-out racism in ugly things I overheard from people attending conferences and camping, and from the community itself. What's useful to speak on are the causes and conditions surrounding my 'resignation.'

There were two health inspections the SMC kitchen had while I was cooking in it. The first one, considering the only instructions I ever received concerned sex and weed, somehow went remarkably well—nailed it! Second one, not so much. Shortly afterward, a new management class began arriving to implement changes to get the kitchen up to code. After a year or so, the existing rules and regulations around food handling were suddenly strenuously enforced; and the kitchen environment, already tense and stressful, became outright oppressive. For me, this was magnified immensely by a predominantly white male staff wagging accusatory fingers at me for not using plastic gloves, while they themselves regularly went in gloveless hands, and worse, let me tell you. The waste that that kitchen produces is abominable.

Whereas at Green Gulch the community was at least having a conversation, nothing at all was being done at SMC regarding diversity and mindfulness around white privilege. Perhaps because there were never more than five black people on staff to begin with, this critical aspect of sangha work simply never happened. Nobody was 'going there,' in any way. Gradually, I started to realize I was in the middle of a corporate purge, when another cook, a colorful, hippie maverick type, 'resigned' after years of being a community member; and then, in an instant, another employee 'resigned.' Upon hearing the details of my fellow cook's highly unpleasant meeting with management, which led to his 'resignation' (firing), I had a creeping feeling I'd probably be next. They were already trumping up (and I mean that at multiple levels) charges of 'insubordination' against me following an incident: a cook, a 19-year-old white kid from Vermont who was also my housemate, had yelled and pointed in my face over some incredibly trivial point of order, with such unhinged gusto that I needed to leave the shift in order to not plaster him all over the walls. If SMC had ever made anything resembling an overture to a race relations dialogue, he might've thought twice about his very unmindful speech and action; but it didn't, and I was forced to face this sort of blind racial insensitivity around the kitchen all the time. As they threatened me with termination, I explained to management that what I'd actually done in leaving the shift was save SMC the grief of trying to explain another 'how did this happen' tragedy nobody could have possibly seen coming, because we weren't discussing, or even thinking about, social justice (or basic manners, for that matter). They accepted it and didn't fire me, but I was pretty sure my head was on the block.

Maybe three or four days later, a Kasung, who's sort of like a cop in Shambhala, pulled me aside and requested that I go home and put on different pants; because—and this is nearly a direct quote—"your dick is disturbing our guests . . . and, oh by the way, other community members have complained about it too." Ahh, so *now* we arrive at the center of the shrubbery maze! Tempted though I am to ascend the soapbox for a scathing polemic on this country and civilization's schizophrenically deadly obsession with the black male body, I'll just say: being told this in such garish language confirmed a deep-seated suspicion of mine about my public presentation and perception, backed by evidence accruing long (no pun intended) before arriving at Shambhala Mountain Center.

I've since heard from a former resident, and the one person there I could call my friend, that the SMC kitchen did indeed tighten up its act. Great! I'm not hating; I honestly hope it works out. There's certainly something profound there. But at the time, after being 'resigned,' nine days before Christmas, from an extraordinarily dysfunctional non-practicing Buddhist community kitchen suddenly scoured clean by a corporate regime, I was feeling some kind of way—not charitable. As I sat in my drafty log cabin room, and wrote yet another letter addressing microaggressions, privilege, and racism, entirely alienated from a mute 'community,' it repeatedly occurred to me how ironic it was to have found Shambhala—the mythical kingdom in the mountains—to in fact be yet another site of insular status-quo Americanism. And yet, somehow, like with my time at Green Gulch, the year and five months living and working there had been a perfect opportunity to contemplate, in solitude, the contemporary social situation as it really is.

Scrambling around in the middle of a season of endings and closures to again avoid homelessness, my thoughts often drifted to the weird placard in the kitchen office that so perplexed and annoyed me when I first arrived. There was no way around it—an exceedingly crazy wisdom was indeed at work at Shambhala Mountain Center; Trungpa Rinpoche's smudgy fingerprints were all over my time there. Trying to remain motivated and sane, I often revisited the verse at the beginning of this chapter, trying to find another way to 'be like water' and learn 'how to blend,' when the temperature drops and water freezes. Cast from 'the perfected kingdom' during a purge in the dead of winter, with eerie howling winds rattling the plasterboard walls, the whole situation required an icy kind of detachment to navigate, an equally calculating and mechanistic resolve. When I was told I'd need to pack my things and leave, out of sheer exasperation, I said aloud to no one in particular: "What would the Buddha have to say about this?" If my depiction in the rhyme was in any way on-point, he'd probably use the incident as a teaching moment, à la some Zen anecdote featuring a snarky monk with clear insight.

I sent the letter to the few residents and senior staff that could be bothered to think about such things. But aside from a few sad remarks of solidarity from community members, the sole response from leadership basically amounted to, "Better luck next time." Well, whether luck or something a little deeper, I decided to follow up on an opportunity a few SMC visitors mentioned I ought to try. Despite having serious doubts, I applied and was accepted, within fifteen days, to a very idiosyncratic, singular, small-but-spirited institution called Naropa University.

Conclusion: 2023

Publisher's Note: The following is an edited transcription of an interview conducted by the editor, Daniel Jami, with the author, Kyva Holman, in November of 2023. When we received the 'completed' manuscript in early 2021 it lacked an effective conclusion, and due to the author's loss of vision, writing such a conclusion outright was off the table. Thus the author and editor were inspired to provide this interview as the only effective way to convey something of an end to this winding narrative in the author's own words. Like the rest of the manuscript, the following has been reviewed and approved by the author after a tedious process of telephonic verbal narration and editing. Given meta observations on this book's construction have been a part of its narrative from the beginning (or as the author would say, from jump), we thought it fitting to provide this insight into our process.

DJ: So at the end of 2015, you left Shambhala Mountain Center, after a falling out, to attend Naropa University in Boulder, Colorado, from where we began this memoir in 2017. Now, here we are in 2023. Can you describe what's happening in your life now?

KH: Can I describe what's happening in my life now? No, probably not . . .

Well, the first thing to say is that I can barely see anything. I'm living at the business end of a long slide toward blindness. My eyesight's pretty far gone; I only have maybe eight or nine percent left. I'm living in a residential hotel on the edge of West Oakland—with helicopters in the air every day, motorcycle gangs buzzing around on their bikes, homeless encampments everywhere, the smell of sewage in the air. Apparently people are dumping their trash on the sidewalk, and just recently, I literally tripped and almost fell into the street, staggering over broken glass and a big wet rag. There's a block right up the street that I have to pass by every day, where they're building a bicycle path and enlarging the sidewalk, that I've fondly come to call 'the corners of confusion.'

Just a couple days ago, I was walking through there and one of the construction guys was leading me to the other side. And when we got there, I said to him, "Look, we need to have a meeting with the mayor; tell her we need a walkway here." See, they had enlarged the street but hadn't painted a walkway, so there's no markers for anybody to safely cross from one side to the other. And he said to me, "Listen bro, not only are you not going to get that, but you don't want to know what's going on out here. You're fortunate you can't see what's going on in this city. Right across the street there's an encampment . . ." and he kept going with this, that, and so forth. So I broke in and said, "You know what man I can't see it, but I can smell it, and I feel it."

Essentially, when people ask me how it is that I'm doing, I tell them, "I'm riding the silvery razor's edge of apocalypse." And that's pretty much what I've been facing full on since I've been here, in this amazing and trying city. Oakland has been trying to cook my goose ever since I got back here, and it's been quite a ride wrestling with that. It's crazy: it reminds me of the term 'Yisra'el,' which means 'wrestling with God,' 'cause this city is definitely a god of some sort. You know that's what cities are—'cities' = 'siddhis (spiritual powers)'—and this city has been exerting its siddhis, its powers against me.

For over seven months, I've had allergy pollen in my eyes every day, and have to stop when I walk outside and put in eye drops, while standing there with my nose running. Things are a complete blur, and it's just racket and funk and tension, drama and disarray around me. So yeah, I'm deeply immersed in and facing the entropy in the world. And believe it or not, I'm having the time of my life, and can't believe how exciting and fabulous and transformative it is. It's both great and terrible, you know? It's like I'm living the ultimate soap opera, and am on the edge of my seat.

DJ: Can you give us some insight into what a typical day might look like for you in this period? How are you spending your time and making ends meet?

KH: Well I'm fundamentally living off of disability. I get SSDI (Social Security Disability Insurance), which gives me $1142 or so a month. That's not a lot to live on, but fortunately enough, the residential hotel I'm staying at isn't charging me rent. This place is actually a lot better than I would have ever imagined this kind of experience being in Oakland. When I first got here, they had fresh blankets, all these toiletries, the room was clean, etc. I'm close to the bathrooms, and there's actually a lot to be thankful for. In a certain way, it's amazing how much my stay here has been indicative of some kind of an evolution in the way the city is dealing with these things. But regardless, I still only have a very small amount of money in my account, so I'm living hand to mouth on this disability salary.

Being a foodie, a lion's share of my budget goes toward my one meal a day. Allowing myself to indulge my foodie habit, I'll go to a nice restaurant I like and eat lunch or dinner. To get around, I've been making use of the e-taxi app Lyft a lot, which has really been working out. I've got this unbelievably dope, top-of-the-line iPhone, that I got from the Department of Rehabilitation, which has really been supporting me. They've been giving me some vocational training, and I think they're setting me up with a laptop. There were people at Naropa who told me this was something I should do, so I signed up with the Department of Rehabilitation, which like I said, has been really supportive with things like mobility and technology training.

So an average day would probably be something like getting up, sitting on the side of the bed, head in my hands like, 'What a mess! What am I gonna do?' Shortly afterward, I'll sort of snap out of it and remember that, you know, I've got another breath, another 24 hours. And the truth of the matter is that as dramatic and terrible as the narrative is, the sensation's quite another thing—it's enough to fuel me for the day.

So what I'll usually do is go and stop at one of the local cafes, drink a bit of coffee, maybe have a bagel with butter and jelly. Then I'll listen to some podcasts and programs, or listen to documentaries ('cause I can't watch 'em), or I'll do some research on Toronto and the University of Toronto, to get used to the idea of living there, as I'm in the process of applying to the university. The entire time, I'm reckoning with the unspeakably insane journey that led me there.

In the afternoon, I might walk around Lake Merritt, an artificial Lake in the middle of Oakland. And while walking, I might end up talking to some people, basically dispensing the Dharma, giving them a vibrational dose of what it's like to have this worked out. Often I'll find a a tree to sit under, and meditate for maybe an hour and a half or two, dealing with all varieties of human reaction to what it is that one sees and feels. My meditation practice includes a variety of techniques: visualization, the basics of *vipassana*, mantras, chanting, intention setting, and choiceless awareness.

Post meditation I'll sometimes go and eat somewhere, making my way across town, wading through screaming fits and arguments. Just a couple days ago somebody unloaded a shotgun over by the lake, and helicopters came; that's just one of many instances of chaos, catastrophe, and mayhem occuring around me daily. At the restaurant, I'll have a little drink and try something new on the menu, and just enjoy or not enjoy what it is that I'm eating, while allowing people to have their experience of me from whatever their viewpoint.

Then I'll come home, and a lot of times I'll just practice the guitar. Fortunately enough, the few possessions I have include musical instruments, so I've gotten quite proficient on the guitar. I'm certainly no Hendrix, no Ernie Eisley or Michael Hampton, but I can play right along with different forms of music. In those moments, it's really a full and total immersion in just how much chaos can produce transcendence. And that's basically what a day in the life looks like now.

O, and when I can remember, I will practice my Yang style tai-chi forms either in a park or in my limited room space, and/or Yoga, even though I don't have a mat and couldn't fit one in this room anyway. As of recently I have also been toying with cannabis astral travel experiments, trying to induce out-of-body experiences to varying degrees of efficacy.

DJ: It sounds like navigating the loss of your eyesight, and accompanying instability of housing, has forced you into a kind of urban-monk lifestyle. Thanks to the combination of the housing resource and disability payments it seems you've got your basic needs met, with the ability to live a simple life and contemplative time on your hands, not wholly unlike the humble life of traditional monastics. Despite the noted challenges of your circumstances, including lacking the supportive context of traditional monasticism, is that a fair characterization?

KH: Yes it is. That's about as neatly and crisply summarized as it could be. I'm literally an urban monk.

DJ: Can we go back a bit now? In 2015, you went to Naropa to finish your undergrad; so how did we get here? Can you summarize the time in Boulder and at Naropa, and how it led to where you are today?

KH: Well I was at Naropa University from the winter of '17 until the spring of '21, when I graduated with a master's degree in religious studies. As you noted, when I first started I was getting a bachelor's degree, which ended up being in interdisciplinary studies and taking me until 2019 to complete. I didn't feel like I was ready to leave the institution at that point, because I didn't really have a plan, partly due to my steadily-worsening eyesight. So I decided to go on to get my master's degree in religious studies, which I completed in the spring of 2021.

The fact Naropa's situated in a town like Boulder is really a testament to the capacity for a Buddhist to visualize and actualize a heavenly *bardo*. The experience in town itself, with its creeks and greenery, paths and waterfalls, was beyond extraordinary. The educational aspect of it all was also extraordinary, but in a much more trying and challenging way.

The statement Trungpa made—"Let East meet West and the sparks will fly"—certainly foreshadowed the many infernos I found myself in, while encountering the school's various permutations of communities. But in line with what the *bodhisattva* is supposed to encounter, overcome, and transform in the suffering world, it provided me with the perfect opportunity to do exactly that kind of transformative work. Despite repeatedly feeling on the outside of any community, I advanced tremendously in my understanding of Buddhism, Hip Hop, Blackness, and this whole business of manifesting in a material form. So the school did exactly what you'd imagine and hope for a Buddhist themed university in the United States. The experience at Naropa put everything about how we got here as a race and species on the table—with all its warts and grotesqueness, foolery and fuckery and brilliance. I had a chance to bathe in it and then rinse it off myself in disgust, time and time again.

After graduating in 2021, I was like 'Alright, now what?' I was there at the Naropa dorm needing to figure out what the hell I was going to do next, when my friend told me I ought to try moving to Costa Rica, where he had lived with family for several years. Finally, after much convincing, I decided to relocate. So with no real plan of where to go, I used a fair chunk of the money that I'd saved through school to fly to Costa Rica, with the intention of living there. Because of financial aid, I had nearly 18k in the bank, the most money I'd ever had. But after an eight-day adventure, filled with a blockbuster movie's worth of misadventures, we failed to find a place for me to relocate, and I came back to Boulder.

Fortunately enough, I was able to sublet the apartment of another friend, Alexis, who was moving. For the next eight months I lived in that tiny apartment in Central Boulder. It was probably only sixteen paces front to back, but was great, even if fantastically small. The layout was quaint, with a fireplace, a little counter for a kitchen, and a little half bathroom. For those months I lived a very spartan and simple, but comfortable life. Alexis and I would go grocery shopping, and get all kinds of gourmet goodies. We'd cook and talk about being foodies and the different ingredients we liked, trading quirky cooking secrets along the way. Sometimes the other homie would also come over and we'd have some good laughs. In its simplicity, it was a version of the way I'm living now in Oakland.

But as it goes, the rent on that place went up, and if I had stayed, it'd have consumed pretty much my entire disability check. So I couldn't stay there anymore, and needed to make a decision. The homie convened a meeting with my two brothers and another friend, all of whom had been in the Subterreanz and Exile Society back in the day. Together we decided I needed to come back to the Bay Area, but let's just say that was not what I wanted to do. I made the decision kicking and screaming, but agreed to it when I was outvoted and out of options.

I touched down in Oakland in June of 2022. For a couple months, I stayed at the Jack London Inn, and then moved into my brother's place for a couple months. My brother's a big restorative-justice sheriff in this town, so with his knowledge and connections at work, he was able to get me 'into the system,' and connected to housing with Bay Area Community Services. They're the organization that's providing this room at the residential hotel where I've been living since August '23.

DJ: Thank you, sounds like it's been quite the journey! Hearing of these experiences makes me curious about your internal mental, emotional, and spiritual state amidst all this. Can you speak to that, and how your present circumstances, and the previous eight years or so, factor into the journey of *vipassanā* or awakening that you've been speaking to throughout the book?

KH: The entire time was a journey through, or rather a page by page reading of, *things as they really are.* Everything about material reality in this postmodern era, and what has been predicted for thousands of years to be an apocalypse, has been laid out. So time and time again, I found myself remembering the importance of bearing in mind that the chaos and clusterfuckery, confusion and calamity, that I was encountering was temporary and, to a certain extent, impersonal and illusory. Interestingly enough, these experiences laid the groundwork for the way I see and experience the world now, in the following sense. The capacity to create events that you can then participate in comes directly out of the moment of seeing that *subject and object are not two.* I had a friend who once said of this mode of experience and perception, "Not same, not separate."

From the time I found myself back in Oakland until now, I've been traveling through the world with increasing confidence and assuredness, as a result of consistently tracking, remembering, appreciating, and engaging with this remarkable dataset that has been accumulating since long before now. It really is an amazing, threadbare, gripping journey from boyhood, to manhood, to spirithood, to godhood.

DJ: It seems like you're speaking to a certain kind of intensification of both hardship and illumination, where side-by-side with increased personal and collective difficulties, there has also been a deepening and clarifying of your spiritual journey and vision. Is that fair?

KH: Yeah, again well put. The bottom line is quite simply that samsara *is* nirvana! It's unbelievable the way the Buddha nailed it, and not only the Buddha, but Goenkaji and Nagarjuna and all of them. You know all the *Daioshos,* gurus, and *Rinpoches,* and so many of these kinds of people have really articulated something fundamental and profound about what it takes to be incarnate. It's so deep! For instance, I've recently been led—shock of all shocks— back to Christianity, Jesus Christ, and the Old Testament, reconsidering with a fresh and entirely unexpected viewpoint, what the true nature of this ancient Hebrew narrative might mean for people who currently classify themselves as foundational black Americans and American descendants of slaves. In essence, I'm a black bodhisattva who has accepted a wild-eyed radical black revolutionary Jesus Christ as his lord and savior, doing the holy work of the original perennial philosophy: out here in these streets on some real shit.

DJ: Speaking of which, what about these identity markers of Black, Buddhist, B-boy; how do you relate to each of those individually and as a hybridized whole at this point in your life?

KH: Each of them is a cipher; each is a scripture.

Blackness, like the other descriptors, has its own ontology; and I'm so deeply immersed in it right now that sometimes it seems I can't be seen. It's funny, it reminds me of something a guy said to me when I was at the Parliament of World Religions in Toronto in 2018. I was rapping for this guy who looked right out of Central Casting, you know. He had his eyes closed while I was rapping, and finally he stopped me and said, "You are the one who sees all, and cannot be seen." And I just kind of exhaled like, 'Roger that, thank you!

Hip Hop just celebrated its 50th anniversary, and I've been invested in the ongoing conversation in the culture about Hip Hop's origins and intentions. There's a brother by the name of Tariq Nasheed who's putting together a documentary called *Microphone Check: The Hidden History of Hip Hop*, where he's making the point that, contrary to what a lot of people are now trying to assert, Hip

Hop came specifically from the people they call 'black' in America. This is of course true of most musical genres originating in America, like rock, jazz, and funk. But aside from these debates on Hip Hop's cultural origination, I've been generally disillusioned with Hip Hop, and have even questioned if it may have been a racket from the jump, rather than being an initially revolutionary force that was later corrupted.

Nonetheless, a Buddhist who has one foot in meditation practice and another in the streets has his torso in a rarefied atmosphere. But my head, when not entangled in disturbing cataclysmic ponderings, heads to a still more rarefied atmosphere that transcends the particularities and limitations of my 'other limbs.' So what I'm realizing now is the intersection of Buddhism, B-boy, and Blackness is in a word 'divinity.' It's the culmination of what it is the Five Percent Nation talked about when they presented the notion of the God—that there's a way of reaching a point of practice where you experience the world exactly as you've designed it to be experienced.

DJ: Boom. Alright then, last question. Side by side with your personal narrative throughout the memoir are your thoughts on our collective life and evolution. Indeed, it seems that for you these things are not separate at all; as you said in the introduction, ". . . this Black Bostonian B-Boy Buddhist in Boulder came to be as the result of encountering a deliberately enlarged sense of 'Self'—a 'Self' that is not the same as, and yet not separate from, the whole." So lay it on us, a final testament to the reader if you will: what do you feel is happening in this larger cosmic self of which we find ourselves partaking?

KH: In case people haven't figured this out, we are living in a time that has been foretold for many hundreds and thousands of years. There's a clashing calamity of clumsy crises, a collective schizophrenia, that has been in the works for many years as a result of peak experiences poorly integrated at a personal and collective level.

Change has indeed come to America, but in so far as African-Americans are concerned, Barack Obama had nothing to do with it whatsoever. I believe there was a Newsweek cover that featured a picture of the president with the caption "The first LGBT president." There's a lot I could say about that, but I will just mention that he did a lot more to advance the causes of that constituency than he ever got close to doing for us. But assuredly Trump was no better, and the trends we saw intensifying during his presidency such as fake news, wild antagonisms between the Left and Right, and other societal tensions have seemingly only gotten worse. At this point, a CGI deep-fake jack-o-lantern with a corn cob pipe and a cardboard party hat could do just about the same job as the Commander in Chief. By the time you factor in climate change, creeping totalitarianism, COVID-19, the Great Reset, AI chatbots, social-media addiction, and performative wokeness, we have some real cataclysmic shit and blood on our hands.

There's a gentleman at the University of Toronto—which *inshallah* (God willing), I am on my way to—named professor John Vervaeke, who speaks about what he calls 'the meaning crisis.' Everything that's going on in the world right now has to do with us having lost sight of what it means to be human, what it means to be suspended between the worlds of the gods and animals. Moreover, rather than losing such insight, most people don't have it to begin with. And tragically, there's a smaller amount of people who have this insight, but use such vision for the purposes of manipulation, control, and fear. But outside the ignorant and evil, there's a smaller subset that understands these things and is trying to make a positive difference. In the Five Percent Nation, they call these people 'the poor righteous teachers.' So people, just know there are poor righteous teachers who persist among the general populace. They don't make a lot of physical noise, but they do make a deep and profound impact on the collective atmosphere. These people are in various locations of identity, but are all harbingers and ambassadors of a way of existing that will come into fruition on the opposite end of what it is that's coming.

The best thing I can say to people who are reading this message is the following. Jesus Christ is a lot of different things to a lot of different people. Instead of debating, arguing and carrying on with each other—about things like, 'Was he divine or human? Was he black or white (though, he was black, of course)? Was he a historical figure or metaphorical character? Is he this or that?'—I would suggest considering Jesus Christ as a form of technology, given the circumstances we find ourselves in today, particularly with AI, the singularity, transhumanism, and so on and so forth. "Jesus Christ" is a way of upgrading your human organic machine to behave in the world in ways that will allow you to transition through what is coming.

Understand that there is a resolution of the duality, the polarization, the angst, the ennui, the fear, the outrage, and the violent disgust that is all too easily held against the world as it is. I have reached a point of equilibrium with this duality that makes me confident equilibrium is possible within the broader context of humanity. Remember, the human race begins in Africa, and since we are all refractions of the initial civilizing impulse there, at the deepest and most profound genetic and biological levels, we have it within ourselves to navigate what it is that we have gotten ourselves into.

Again, I want to say that the three factors to be looking for as we go forward are: natural consequences, ripening karma, and boundary dissolution. Get used to it; it's expected; figure out a way to love it because it's happening. If you're playing a game—and we did go over *tha Game* in this book—realize just how deeply it really is a game. Those of us who are dealing with Hip Hop and new understandings of it will have to confront, remember, acknowledge, and come to grips with having been subjected to that particular game. Hip Hop, after all, is just one of many different subgames within 'the game of life' itself. There's a whole philosophy about this called 'Game Theory,' which deals with how the different aspects of a system interact and engage with each other to allow an organism to manifest, grow, and reproduce.

The question humanity faces right now is: What are you going to produce? What are you going to reproduce?

Personally, I'm not interested in 'products.' There are panacea products being advertised everywhere, but that's not what I'm talking about. My question is: what can you produce on behalf of the effort of human liberation? That's my clarion call to the audience. Take it from your new Buddhist friend, who's had the opportunity to traverse the universe, come back, and find out that we are both everything and everyone and nothing at all . . .

DJ: Period?

KH: Period.

DJ: It seems like there's only one way to end it. Let's hit 'em with:

> . . . *We'll be haunting you along with the* dralas.
> *Jolly good luck!*

KH: Lol! *Word is bond.*